STORIES OF CIVIL WAR SONGS

Stories of
Civil War Songs

by

ERNEST K. EMURIAN

Author of

Plays and Pageants for Many Occasions
More Plays and Pageants for Many Occasions
Living Stories of Famous Hymns
Famous Stories of Inspiring Hymns
Stories of Our National Songs
Stories of Christmas Carols
Living Stories of Favorite Songs
Ten New Plays for Church and School
Forty True Stories of Famous Gospel Songs
Stories of Yuletide

W. A. Wilde Company   Natick, Mass.

Copyright 1960, by
W. A. WILDE COMPANY

All rights reserved

STORIES OF CIVIL WAR SONGS

Library of Congress Catalog Card Number 60-15262

Printed in U.S.A.

To
The Memory of
My Mother's Grandfather
Rev. Albert G. Ruliffson
Founder of The Bowery Mission
in
New York City
and
A Member of
The United States Christian Commission
During the War of 1861-1865

PREFACE

The Civil War ended in 1865, and a little more than a quarter of a century later, twenty-seven years to be exact, in 1892, Rev. Francis Bellamy, a distinguished Baptist clergyman associated with "The Youth's Companion" magazine in Boston, wrote "The Pledge of Allegiance to the American Flag" to be used in connection with Columbus Day celebrations throughout the nation in October of that year, during which exercises American flags were to be raised above more than twenty-five thousand schoolhouses in the country. The Pledge, as originally written by Mr. Bellamy, contained these words, "I pledge allegiance to my flag, and to the Republic for which it stands; one nation, indivisible, with liberty and justice for all."

A little more than a quarter of a century later, twenty-six years to be exact, in 1918, the armistice which brought an end to the First World War was signed, and a little more than a quarter of a century after that historic event, twenty-seven years later to be exact, in 1945, the Second World War came to an end. These conflicts broke out mainly because the people of the world had not yet come to the place where they were willing to salute a universal flag with the words "one world, indivisible."

Twenty-seven years from the close of the Second World War will bring us to the year 1972. If by that time we have not learned to say "one world, indivisible" and a Third World War breaks out, more than likely there will be no one left to write any songs, no one left to sing any songs and nothing left worth singing about!

Ernest K. Emurian
Elm Avenue Methodist Church, Portsmouth, Va.

CONTENTS

DIXIE

The only thing southern about the song "Dixie" is its title and subject matter because the author and composer, Daniel Decatur Emmett (1815-1904), was a native of the northern state of Ohio who wrote his popular minstrel song in the northern state of New York two years prior to the assault on Fort Sumter which marked the beginning of the War Between The States. The grandson of a Revolutionary War hero and the son of a veteran of the War of 1812, Daniel was given his middle name "Decatur" because one of his father's heroes was Commodore Stephen Decatur (1779-1820) of the United States Navy, whose famous toast, delivered in Norfolk, Virginia in April, 1816, was typical of the patriotism of those turbulent times, "Our country! In her intercourse with foreign nations may she always be in the right; but our country, right or wrong!"

As soon as he learned to read, young Daniel, who was born in Mount Vernon, Ohio, October 29, 1815, the year after Francis Scott Key wrote "The Star Spangled Banner," got a job as a "printer's devil" on the local newspaper, writing up local news and doing some proof-reading on the side, while his father farmed a small piece of land nearby and ran the village blacksmith shop in his spare time. What music he knew he learned at his mother's knee, and, when the opportunity presented itself later on, he mastered several musical instruments including the piano, violin, trumpet, flute, fife and drum. In fact, he joined the United States Army as a fifer, and was stationed briefly at Newport, Kentucky and St. Louis before being discharged because of his youth. He must have become confused about his real age and possibly exaggerated it a bit when he enlisted, imagining himself older than he actually was! Anyway, he learned a lot about military music during his brief enlistment, and it stood him in good stead some years later when he utilized the results of that experience in his compositions.

His first successful song was written in 1830 when Daniel was a young stripling of fifteen, and was typical of the others he was to write in the years ahead. Entitled "Old Dan Tucker," and set to a jiggy tune, the young poet-composer wrote:

1. I came to town de udder night, I heard de noise, den
       saw de sight;
   De watchmen dey was runnin' roun', Cryin' 'Ole Dan
       Tucker's come to town.'

   Chorus:

   Git outen de way, get outen de way, Get outen de way,
       Ole Dan Tucker,
   You's too late to come to your supper.

2. Sheep an' hog awalkin' in de pasture, Sheep says, 'Hog,
       can't you go faster?'
   'Hush, hush, honey, hear de wolf growlin', Ah, ah, Lawd,
       de bull dog growlin'.'

The next few years were spent with travelling circuses where Emmett made quite a reputation for himself as an entertainer, soon graduating from the "big top" to vaudeville. Now a seasoned professional, Daniel drifted to New York City where a sudden flash of inspiration one night led him to blacken his face with burnt cork and take the part of a Negro in his act, thus, unwittingly, giving birth to the blackface minstrel which set a standard for public entertainment that lasted more than three quarters of a century. He later organized his own troupe of "Virginia Minstrels" and even took them on a successful tour of England. On his return to the United States, Emmett became associated with Bryant's Minstrels, working closely with Jerry, Neil and Dan Bryant in the production of their shows that packed Mechanics' Hall at 472 Broadway, near Grand Street, New York City, night after night. It was late on Saturday night, September 17,

12

1859, that Dan and Jerry Bryant knocked at the door of Emmett's room in a cheap boarding house on New York's Catherine Street. Dan and his wife had not yet retired, and soon the four of them were talking excitedly about the need for a new song for the following Monday night's performance. The Bryant brothers suggested that a peppy "walk-around" would liven up the show considerably, an observation with which Mr. and Mrs. Emmett agreed. Before the brothers returned to their room upstairs on the next floor, the forty-four year old performer and composer had agreed to do what he could as quickly as possible.

The next day, Sunday, September 18, was as dismal and dreary as a day could be, and the Emmetts were compelled to stay indoors all day. Daniel, longing for some sunshine and a breath of fresh air to help brush the cobwebs out of his brain so he could get to work on the new song, sat around and moped during the long morning hours, finally turning to his wife and saying, "Honey, I wish I was in Dixie, way down in the sunny south." Soon they were talking about their experiences in Charleston and Memphis and New Orleans, and the other southern cities they had visited numbers of times. Then their conversation turned to reminiscences of scenes of lazy living along the Mississippi, the Colonels and their lovely ladies sipping juleps in the blue-grass region of Kentucky, and darkies chopping cotton near Savannah or lifting huge bales of "white gold" on to the barges at Vicksburg, or chanting their mournful spirituals in the cool of an evening outside their humble cabin doors back of the huge mansions that graced many a spacious plantation in the deep south. Emmett rather casually added, "I'd swap all of New York City for another day in Dixie," and immediately his wife interrupted him by saying, "There's the theme for your new song, Dan. Write a song about the sunny south, about Dixie!" So the man who had been born in Ohio sat down at a desk in his room in New York City that rainy afternoon, September 18, 1859, and conjured up memories of the southland and began to write the song that was to become the marching hymn of the Confederacy before the end of the next two years.

13

Some folks say that the word "Dixie" was a corruption of Dixon, taken from the name of one of the two surveyors, Mason and Dixon, who surveyed that famous "Mason-Dixon" line of demarcation between the northern and southern states, while others insist that it came from the name of a French piece of paper money used in New Orleans, a "dix" or a "ten spot," rich folks being called "dix-es" since they had a lot of those pieces of currency in their possession. Still others say that once upon a time there was a land owner on Manhattan Island named Mr. Dixey (or Dixie) who treated his slaves with such respect that when they were shipped south and resold after New York state passed a law outlawing slavery after 1822, they spoke longingly of "going back to Mr. Dixie's" a strange new word their illiterate co-workers took over as just plain "Dixie," which soon came to be symbolic of a place of peace, security and happiness. Anyway, regardless of its origin or derivation, by 1859 Dixie meant the south, and the south was called Dixieland. In fact, after Dan Emmett's new song became a success and the war broke out, he was almost lynched by an angry mob on the grounds of being a "southern sympathizer" or a "Confederate spy," the proof being that he had written and composed the rebel's most popular war-song, "Dixie" ! He began his new walk-around with a verse about:

Dis worl' was made in jiss six days an' finished up in various ways,

Look away, look away, look away, Dixie land.

Den dey made Dixie trim and nice, but Adam called it "Paradise,"

Look away, look away, look away, Dixie land.

But he soon discarded that, since he thought some folks would regard it as a bit too sacreligious, and began all over again, and soon had another opening stanza down on paper. He recalled later that when the idea hit him, he "jumped up, took his tin whistle and sat down to the table to write. In less than an hour he had the first verse and chorus." His wife wisely left him to his own thoughts and spent the rest of that memorable afternoon with friends in another part

14

of the boarding house. When he finished his new song, he read over these stanzas:

1. I wish I was in de lann ob cotton, Ole times darr am not
       forgotten,
   Look away, look away, look away, Dixie land;
   In Dixie lann whar I was bawn in, Arly on one frosty
       mawnin',
   Look away, look away, look away, Dixie land.

   Chorus:

   Den I wish I was in Dixie! Hooray! Hooray!
   In Dixie land we'll take our stand to lib and die in Dixie;
   Away, away, away down south in Dixie;
   Away, away, away down south in Dixie.

2. In Dixie lann de darkies grow, If white folks only plant
       deyre toe;
   Look away, look away, look away, Dixie land.
   Dey wet de grown' wid 'bakker smoke, Den up de darkies
       heads will poke,
   Look away, look away, look away, Dixie land.
3. I used to hoe an' dig de lann, But work dey say is con-
       tribann',
   Look away, look away, look away, Dixie land;
   Driber he come pokin' 'bout, when Massa sole me out-
       and-out,
   Look away, look away, look away, Dixie land.
4. Ole Missus die, she took a decline, Her face was de color
       ob bacon-rhine;
   Look away, look away, look away, Dixie land;
   To Kingdom kum den let 'er go, For here on earth she
       stood no show,
   Look away, look away, look away, Dixie land.
5. Buckwheat cakes with cornmeal batter Makes you fat or
       a little fatter,
   Look away, look away, look away, Dixie land;
   Den here's a health to de next ole missus, An' all de gals
       dat want to kiss us,
   Look away, look away, look away, Dixie land.

6. Den hoe it down an' scratch yoa grabble, To Dixie lann
    I'm boun' to trabble,
   Look away, look away, look away, Dixie land;
   Whar de rake an' hoe got double trigger, An' white man
    jiss as good as nigger!
   Look away, look away, look away, Dixie land.

As later polished and perfected for publication, Emmett's
stanzas read as follows:

2. Old Missus marry "Will-de-weaber," Willium was a gay
    deceaber;
   Look away, look away, look away, Dixie land;
   But when he put his arm around 'er, He smiled as fierce
    as a forty pounder,
   Look away, look away, look away, Dixie land.
3. His face was sharp as a butcher's cleaber, But dat did not
    seem to greab 'er,
   Look away, look away, look away, Dixie land;
   Old Missus acted de foolish part, And died for a man dat
    broke her heart,
   Look away, look away, look away, Dixie land.
4. Now here's a health to the next old Missus, An all de gals
    dat want to kiss us,
   Look away, look away, look away, Dixie land;
   But if you want to drive 'way sorrow, Come and hear dis
    song tomorrow,
   Look away, look away, look away, Dixie land.
5. Dar's buckwheat cakes an Ingen' batter, Makes you fat
    or a little fatter,
   Look away, look away, look away, Dixie land;
   Den hoe it down and scratch your grabble,
   To Dixie's land I'm bound to trabble,
   Look away, look away, look away, Dixie land.

The very next night, Monday, September 19, 1859, Emmett
introduced "Dixie" to a packed house at Mechanics' Hall
and discovered that he had almost spontaneously written an
instantaneous success!! He later sold all his rights to the
new song for $300.00 to Firth, Pond and Company, Music

Publishers, 547 Broadway, who printed it on June 21, 1860 and sold it all over the country. By January of 1861 it was being sung as far south as New Orleans.

When plans were being formulated for the inauguration of Jefferson Davis as the first President of the Confederate States of America, in Montgomery, Alabama, Mr. Herman Arnold, a naturalized German musician, cornetist, orchestra and band director from Memphis, who had married a Montgomery girl, was asked to take charge of the music for the occasion. He was looking for an appropriate new selection for his band to play, since most of the traditional pieces were "northern" or "Yankee" tunes and therefore not suitable for this particular auspicious occasion, when his wife rather casually remarked, "Why don't you play that minstrel piece about Dixie's land? It's lively and catchy and would make a good band number." Herman very hurriedly arranged the new song for his band, rehearsed them in a room of the Capitol that had been reserved for the musicians and played "Dixie" as a band number shortly thereafter when President Davis took his oath of office, Monday, February 18, 1861. Few who listened to it that memorable afternoon knew that it had been composed by a northern minstrel man in a northern metropolis, while those who did didn't care, because "Dixie" happened to be just what the new nation needed at that time, and without a thought as to its origin, the southerners took it to their hearts and made it their very own. The Baltimore *Sun* later declared, "Even if it were written by the son of an Abolitionist, 'Dixie' is essentially a plantation song supposedly sung by slaves."

But Emmett was to suffer because of his southern success. His father had been a red-hot abolitionist himself and had been an early organizer of the "underground railroad" that aided many runaway slaves in their flights to freedom, and the composer was soon to receive many letters from northern sympathizers upbraiding him for being a traitor to his country and harshly criticizing him for being unfaithful to the Union. This unfair animosity even made it difficult for the entertainer to earn a decent living during the years of the Civil War, although he did open a music hall in Chicago during the 1870s which enjoyed some success. Eventually he returned to Ohio and operated a small farm not far from his birthplace, Mount Vernon, raising vegetables and chickens for the townsfolk near by, he and his family living in semi-seclusion out in the country. Of his song, he said, "If I had known it was going to become so popular, I would have written it better."

Another minstrel man, Al G. Field, who had once been Emmett's protege, "rediscovered" his old teacher just before the turn of the twentieth century, and insisted on taking him back on the stage to present him to the re-united American people as the author and composer of "Dixie." Wherever the aged showman went he was received with enthusiastic ovations, as the citizens of the United States both north and south tried in this way to atone for the sins of their fathers. It was then that Emmett said, "True, I wrote 'Dixie' and made it popular on the stage; but it was a southern musician who arranged it for his band and gave it to the world." The poverty of his declining years was alleviated by an allowance which the Actor's Fund of New York city granted him.

On June 28, 1904, at the ripe old age of eighty-eight years and eight months, Daniel Decatur Emmett, the northern boy who had written "the battle hymn of the south" in a northern city, passed away and was buried in Mound View Cemetery, Mount Vernon, Ohio, the Elks having charge of the funeral and a band softly playing "Dixie" as his casket was lowered into the grave, the only Yankee ever to be buried to the strains of Confederate music. One of the finest tributes paid Emmett and his song was this, "When a southerner comes home with calloused hands, he has either been plowing or applauding 'Dixie'!"

THE BATTLE HYMN OF THE REPUBLIC

During the early summer of 1852 a young musician and song leader from Richmond, Virginia, William Steffe by name, travelled south to lead the music in an old-fashioned Georgia camp meeting. When he arrived on the scene, he discovered to his surprise that there were no song books available, since, according to the director of the camp meeting, "The folks who sing can't read and the folks who read can't sing so why bother with song books?"

When he learned he would either have to "line out" some old hymns and favorite gospel songs or write his own new ones, he was undaunted and set himself to the task with all the enthusiasm and talent he could muster. Steffe was enough of a musician to realize that the popularity of the spirituals of the southern Negro was mainly due to the constant repetition of the principal theme in addition to the fact that, in many instances, the music of the Chorus was that of the stanzas as well. With that in mind, he decided to create some hymn-spirituals of his own, built around those truths which most of the people who attended a camp meeting held in common with nearly everybody else. In order to eliminate any thought of controversy, he penned the most popular of his original songs on the subject of "Heaven," repeating the first line three times before adding a fourth and final line, arranging his melody around three basic chords, so he could strum them on his guitar if necessary. As he ultimately wrote this gospel hymn down, the three stanzas contained these simple lines:

1. Say, brothers, will you meet us,
   Say, brothers, will you meet us,
   Say, brothers, will you meet us
   On Canaan's happy shore?

2. By the grace of God we'll meet you,
   By the grace of God we'll meet you,
   By the grace of God we'll meet you
   On Canaan's happy shore.
3. Jesus lives and reigns forever,
   Jesus lives and reigns forever,
   Jesus lives and reigns forever,
   On Canaan's happy shore.

When he got to the Chorus, he recalled an expression that was all the vogue at that time, among white people as well as Negroes, and, to the same stirring rhythm of the stanzas he sang the words of this Refrain:

Glory, glory hallelujah,
Glory, glory hallelujah,
Glory, glory hallelujah,
For ever, evermore.

Little realizing that he had stumbled upon a "natural" that was soon to sweep the country, and, to other and nobler stanzas was to become the marching hymn of the north during the trying and tragic years of the Civil War, southern-born William Steffe, a Richmonder, introduced his new song at that Georgia camp meeting and was both pleased and thrilled at the response of the people.

Some of his friends commented, "There's no end to a song like that, William, for we can start with 'Say, sister, will you meet us?' and go on to 'Say, Deacon, will you meet us?' and 'Say, cousin, will you meet us?' and end up with 'Say, Bishop, will you meet us On Canaan's happy shore?' "

As rapidly as any song has ever been accepted by the American people, "Glory, glory hallelujah" was taken to the bosom of the entire nation. Citizens who did not know where the sovereign state of Georgia was, and choristers who had never heard the name of William Steffe sang it as enthusiastically as the rest, and accepted it in the same spirit with which they had embraced the popular ballads of Stephen Foster, and made it their very own. When the southern branch of divided American Methodism, known officially

20

as The Methodist Episcopal Church, South (prior to their eventual reunion in 1939) published a new hymnal in 1889, Hymn number 899 was "Say, Brothers, Will You Meet Us?" In Dr. Wilbur Fiske Tillett's "Annotated Edition" of that volume, this note appears, "This hymn was very popular at revivals many years ago. It will recall to many old Methodists incidents of his early days when people sung more with the spirit than with the understanding."

Connecticut-born John Brown, who in his mature years looked like the reincarnation of an Old Testament prophet, "swore eternal enmity against the evil of slavery" and was willing to shed his own blood as well as that of his family and friends to achieve that end. He actually brought on an anti-slavery riot in Missouri after he moved west, and among the casualties was one of his own sons, but when the self-appointed liberator held off half a thousand pro-slavery fighters with only fifteen men in what historians call "The Battle of Osawatomie," he earned the nickname that followed him to the gallows, "Osawatomie Brown." In need of arms for his forth-coming Armageddon against entrenched slavery, Brown assaulted a well-stocked United States arsenal at Harper's Ferry, Virginia on October 16, 1859. With only twenty-two zealous disciples as his army, he seized the defense-less town and then captured the arsenal. Aroused towns-people, however, instead of falling in line behind Brown, besieged him and his little party in the building, denouncing them as traitors. A company of Marines under Colonel Robert E. Lee was quickly ordered up from Washington to subdue the raiders. In the ensuing battle, ten of Brown's men, including two of his sons, were slain, while only five managed to escape. The remaining seven were taken prisoner, among them the fifty-nine-year-old prophet-patriot himself. He was given as fair a trial as could be granted under the circumstances, for "treason, conspiring with slaves and other rebels and murder in the first degree" while his conviction was a foregone conclusion even before the actual trial got under way. A month and a half after his ill-fated expedition, John Brown was publicly hanged, December 2, 1859, the

21

manner in which he met his death earning him the respect of thousands who rejected his method of attacking the problem of slavery.

When Fort Sumter was fired upon on April 12, 1861 and war burst in all its wild fury over the divided land, the volunteers and conscripts of the northern states began to sing almost spontaneously a new song about the martyred hero John Brown, to the tune of William Steffe's southern camp meeting song, and into their singing they poured all their pent-up hatred of slavery and war, as well as all of their dreamed-up idealism of youth, making it almost a battle hymn as they sang:

1. John Brown's body lies a-mouldering in the grave,
   John Brown's body lies a-mouldering in the grave,
   John Brown's body lies a-mouldering in the grave,
   His soul goes marching on.
      Glory, glory hallelujah!
      Glory, glory hallelujah!
      Glory, glory hallelujah!
      His soul goes marching on.

Subsequent stanzas began with these lines:

2. He's gone to be a soldier in the army of the Lord.
3. John Brown's knapsack is strapped upon his back.
4. His pet lambs will meet him on the way.

Then, while southerners were singing in retaliation, to the same stirring tune:
   We'll hang Abe Lincoln to a sour apple tree,
the Federals countered by singing of the President of the Confederacy:
   We'll hang Jeff Davis to a sour apple tree,
concluding with this admonition:
   Now for the Union we will give three rousing cheers, As
      they go marching on!

Most wars are started in the high hopes that they will be successfully completed within a fortnight, and the Civil War was no exception. When General McClellan mustered his

22

forces for the march to Richmond, the Federals fully expected to brush aside General Beauregard's Confederates with little effort. But when the First Battle of Manassas (Bull Run) was joined on July 21, 1861, he learned differently. In fact, the Yankees were not only stopped dead in their tracks but driven back to the safe side of the Potomac River. While President Lincoln hourly expected an anticipated Confederate invasion of Washington which never came to pass because he did not know by what a small margin the victory had been achieved, he hastily summoned every available soldier to the defense of the capital. As these men passed through New York, Philadelphia, Baltimore and the beleaguered city itself, they marched to the cadences of "Glory, Glory Hallelujah!" and by the time they took their places on the ramparts of Washington, nearly every northern sympathizer was singing the new song with contagious zeal, as they urged their comrades in arms to win the victory they had been promised their sacrifices would assure.

During her long life of ninety-one years, Julia Ward Howe (1819-1910) never presented arms or shouldered a musket, but that she inspired thousands of men to do so cannot be denied, for this woman who was never drafted into the army penned as thrilling a patriotic hymn as has ever been written on American soil. Born in New York city on May 27, 1819, Julia married Dr. Samuel Gridley Howe, the head of Boston's Perkins Institute for the Blind, and twenty years her senior, in 1843. After spending two years abroad, the Howes returned to Boston, and became active members of the abolitionist movement, counting among their close friends such public anti-slavery figures as William Lloyd Garrison and Wendell Phillips.

When the war broke out, Dr. Howe was too old for active duty, so he accepted a position with the Sanitary Commission (Medical Corps), using his skill to bind up the wounded and assist the disabled. In November, 1861, the Howes, accompanied by her pastor and friend, Dr. James Freeman Clarke, travelled from their Boston home at 13 Chestnut Street, to Washington, to see for themselves what the war was all about. On November 21, 1861, with many other sight-seers, they crossed the Potomac to watch a review of Federal troops at nearby Munson Hill Farm, only to find the maneuvers suddenly interrupted by a surprise Confederate attack. The drive home to safety over roads now crowded with a retreating army was a nightmare, and, to nerve some of the stragglers and run-aways to turn and face the enemy, Mrs. Howe began to sing "Glory, Glory Hallelujah!" Soon some of the soldiers took up the strains of the familiar chorus and sang them with such fervor that their retreat became an orderly withdrawal rather than a rout. Rev. Mr. Clarke, sensing the hidden possibilities in the song, turned to his hostess and said, "Mrs. Howe, why don't you write new words to that good air?" To humor him she replied, "Dr. Clarke, I have often wished that I could do that very thing."

Late that night in their room in Washington's Willard Hotel, all the longings, hopes, aspirations and dreams shared by thousands of her fellow Americans crept through the heart and mind of forty-two-year-old Julia Ward Howe, and came to sharp focus as the music of the afternoon kept ringing in her soul. Seeing from their hotel window the "watch fires of a hundred circling camps" and hearing during the night "the trumpet that shall never call retreat," the poet began to picture the war as a holy crusade against everything evil, regarding it with the same distorted religious sanctity and fervor which had characterized the Crusades of the Middle Ages. Soon the sleepless woman picked up a piece of paper, found pen and ink, and began to write. After creating five stanzas to match the tune of "John Brown's Body," she knew she had accomplished her purpose, whereupon she went to bed and fell asleep. Her five stanzas, first published in the February 1862 issue of "The Atlantic Monthly," contained these stirring lines:

1. Mine eyes have seen the glory of the coming of the Lord;
    He is trampling out the vintage where the grapes of wrath
        are stored;
    He hath loosed the fateful lightning of his terrible swift
        sword,
    His truth is marching on.

24

2. I have seen him in the watch-fires of a hundred circling
      camps;
   They have builded him an altar in the evening dews and
      damps;
   I can read his righteous sentence by the dim and flaring
      lamps;
   His day is marching on.
3. I have read a fiery gospel writ in burnished rows of steel,
   "As ye deal with my contemners, so with you my grace
      shall deal;
   Let the hero born of woman crush the serpent with his
      heel";
   Our God is marching on.
4. He hath sounded forth the trumpet that shall never call
      retreat;
   He is sifting out the hearts of men before his judgment
      seat;
   So be swift my soul to answer him, be jubilant, my feet!
   Our God is marching on.
5. In the beauty of the lilies Christ was born across the sea,
   With a glory in his bosom that transfigures you and me;
   As he died to make men holy, let us die to make men free,
   While God is marching on!

When the poem was first published, the words of the
Chorus were omitted, the editor of the journal, Mr. James T.
Fields, concluding that people intelligent enough to read
that magazine would recognize the fact that the refrain could
consist only of the words "Glory, Glory Hallelujah" coupled
with the last line of each stanza. He sent the poet $4 for her
stanzas; at that rate she received eighty cents a stanza, or
about two cents a word!

Among those who learned the hymn was Rev. (Chaplain)
Charles Cardwell McCabe, a Methodist minister from Ohio
who had been captured by the Confederates at Winchester,
Virginia, in 1863 when he was serving with the 122nd Ohio
Volunteer Infantry. For five months he was incarcerated with
thousands of fellow prisoners in Richmond's notorious Libby
Prison. When word of the northern victory at Gettysburg

reached the veterans within the walls, McCabe recalled the lines he had memorized from *The Atlantic Monthly* and taught them to his fellow-prisoners, leading them all in singing "The Battle Hymn Of The Republic." After his release, he sang it all over the country in connection with his famous lecture "The Bright Side Of Life In Libby Prison," the proceeds of his talks going to the Church Extension needs of the Methodist Church. On February 2, 1864, he sang it at a meeting in the Hall of the House of Representatives in Washington and President Lincoln, standing nearby, was so thrilled that he shouted, when the Chaplain finished, "Sing it again!" McCabe sang it again at a memorial service for the assassinated Chief Executive in Springfield, Ohio, in May, 1865.

Mrs. Howe in her later years received many well-deserved honors, and kept busy with literary activities and labors on behalf of prison reform and world peace, preaching occasionally in Unitarian pulpits. Brown University conferred upon her the honorary degree of Doctor of Laws on June 16, 1909, Smith College following suit on October 5, 1910, just twelve days before her death at her Newport, Rhode Island, home "marching to brave music still."

THE BATTLE CRY OF FREEDOM

Three days after Fort Sumter was fired upon, April 12, 1861, President Lincoln issued his first call for troops in a document dated Monday, April 15, 1861, for the purpose of restraining "combinations too powerful to be suppressed by ordinary procedure of government." The paper read in part, "Now, therefore, I, Abraham Lincoln, President of the United States, in virtue of the power in me vested by the Constitution and the laws, have thought fit to call forth, and hereby do call forth, the militia of the several States of the Union, to the aggregate number of seventy-five thousand, in order to suppress said combinations and to cause the laws to be duly executed."

When the Chicago music publisher, composer and teacher, George Frederick Root (1820-1895) heard the news of the assault on Fort Sumter and the President's call for soldiers to suppress the rebellion, he immediately dashed off the first new song of the war, "The First Gun Is Fired, May God Protect The Right."

Since the available and eligible men of the northern states were rather reluctant to respond to their Chief Executive's "call to arms" in great numbers, but merely trickled in to defend their borders and frontiers, the President was compelled to issue a new proclamation, dated May 3, 1861, in which he called into active service 42,034 three-year volunteers, 22,714 enlisted men and 18,000 seamen, thereby enlarging the army to more than 150,000 men, and the navy to over 25,000. When that story was telegraphed throughout the country, George F. Root was visiting in the Chicago home of his brother, E. T. Root, who, with C. T. Cady, had organized the music publishing firm of Root and Cady three years earlier, in 1858. The truth of the matter is that on that memorable afternoon, George was actually "reclining on a lounge" in his brother's home when he heard of the Presidential proclamation. Almost instantly he thought of the flag that had fallen at Fort Sumter, and just as spontaneously these words, together with a suitable martial tune, flashed into his mind:

Yes, we'll rally round the flag, boys, we'll rally once again,
Shouting the battle-cry of freedom!

He spent the rest of the afternoon and evening "thinking out" the new song, and the next morning he wrote it down, both words and music, in his office on the second floor of Root and Cady's publishing house, little realizing that he had just composed what was to become one of the most popular songs of the War Between the States. Those who knew Root were not surprised at the rapid way he turned out popular songs, for, behind the apparent spontaneity which characterized the composing of this and other original songs he was to write during the four years of the Civil War, were fourteen years of hard work and faithful, diligent practice.

The composer himself admitted that "such work as I could do at all, I could do quickly," attributing this to the fact that he had spent many years, "extemporizing melodies on the blackboard, before classes that could be kept in order only by prompt and rapid movements."

Root was born in Sheffield, Massachusetts, August 20, 1820, his family moving to North Reading, not far from Boston, when he was six years of age. During his early adolescence he revealed an aptitude for music which led his parents to entrust his training and development to Mr. A. N. Johnson of Boston. In addition to mastering various musical instruments, Root studied piano under Johnson and voice with George James Webb, a prominent organist and vocal instructor, whose hymn tune "Webb," originally composed for a popular song, " 'Tis Dawn, The Lark Is Singing" is now universally associated with the stirring stanzas of Rev. George Duffield's hymn, "Stand Up, Stand Up For Jesus." Root later spoke of Webb as "an elegant organist, accomplished musician and model Christian gentleman."

Here too he came in contact with Isaac Baker Woodbury (1819-1858) another leading teacher and composer, whose hymn tune "Eucharist" is sometimes wedded with Dr. Isaac Watts' hymn "When I Survey The Wondrous Cross," and Dr. Lowell Mason (1792-1872), the Father of American hymnology and public school music, whose popular tunes for "Nearer, My God, To Thee," "My Faith Looks Up To Thee," and many other hymns are found in almost every Christian hymnal today.

As he learned more, Root began to instruct those coming along behind him, and soon was developing choral clubs, classes and societies in and around the Massachusetts metropolis. He left Boston in 1844 to become the organist of "The Church of the Strangers" on Mercer Street in New York City. In addition to his Church duties there, he conducted classes in various nearby institutions including Union

Theological Seminary (where one of his students was C. T. Cady, later to become a partner with George's brother, E. T. Root, in the Chicago publishing firm of Root and Cady), Rutgers Female Institute and the New York Institute For The Blind, where one of his most famous pupils was Fanny Crosby (1820-1915) the blind poet who wrote the libretto for his first big musical success "The Flower Queen" published in 1852, and who was to become Christendom's most prolific author of gospel hymns and songs. The year after he moved to New York, he married Mary Olive Woodman, who was also an accomplished musician and singer, the wedding being solemnized in August, 1845. In 1850, Root went abroad, spending almost a year studying in Paris. In 1852 he signed a three-year contract with the New York publishing house of William Hall and Son, and they brought out his first successful popular song, "Hazel Dell," that same year. Despite the fact that it was a funereal type of song in the style of "The Letter Edged In Black" and "The Baggage Coach Ahead," although not quite as depressing as those other two, it became quite popular. The first stanza sets the mood for the song in these words:

1. In the Hazel Dell my Nelly's sleeping, Nelly loved so long;
   And my lonely, lonely watch I'm keeping, Nelly lost and gone.
   Here in moonlight often we have wandered, Through the silent shade,
   Now where leafy branches drooping downward, Little Nelly's laid.

Chorus:

All alone my watch I'm keeping, In the Hazel Dell;
For my darling Nelly's near me sleeping, Nelly dear, farewell.

Root admitted that he hesitated to have such songs published under his real name, so he used as his pen name the German translation of his last name, and called himself "G. Frederick Wurzel." Before his contract with the New Yorkers expired, he selected six other popular compositions

29

and offered to sell them to Mr. Hall for $100 each, or a grand total of $600 for all six. Hall demurred, and agreed to publish them on a straight royalty basis. When he turned over a check for $3,000 to the composer the next year as royalties on one of those six songs alone, he confessed that "$600 for the lot would not have been an unreasonable price." That best seller was entitled "Rosalie, The Prairie Flower," another "Wurzel" hit, which told a story like this:

1. On the distant prairie, where the heather wild, In its quiet
    beauty lived and smiled,
   Stands a little cottage and a creeping vine Loves around its
    porch to twine.
   In that peaceful dwelling was a lovely child, With her
    blue eyes beaming soft and mild,
   And the wavy ringlets of her flaxen hair, Waving in the
    summer air.

Chorus:

Fair as a lily, joyous and free, Light of that prairie home
    was she;
Everyone who knew her felt the gentle power of Rosalie,
    the Prairie Flower.

Root always referred to his first gospel song, "Come to The Saviour," in the words of the prominent lay evangelist Dwight L. Moody, who spoke of it glowingly as the "Rally Round The Flag" of the gospel!

One day while Root was working at his Willow Farm home near North Reading, Massachusetts, his mother passed through the room and handed him a slip of paper which she had just clipped from a religious journal she had been reading, and said, "George, I think that would be good for music." As he read over the simple stanzas, a melody formed in his mind, and soon he completed the music for his popular sacred song "The Shining Shore." As he harmonized the melody the following day, he realized that it was quite commonplace, but decided that it might be useful nevertheless and the response of those who sang it and heard it justified

30

his faith in the new song. The growth of the Chicago music publishing firm of Root and Cady led George to sever his connections in New York and move with his wife and their five children to the Illinois city in 1863, by which time he was already being regarded as the most successful composer of Civil War songs.

All of these years of learning, studying, teaching, instructing, playing, versifying and composing enabled George F. Root to dash off his songs with almost effortless ease, and that May morning in 1861 saw him putting the finishing touches on his new war song in his Chicago office and checking the music manuscript carefully before setting it to one side. His original four stanzas and Chorus were these:

1. Yes, we'll rally round the flag, boys, we'll rally once again,
   Shouting the battle-cry of freedom;
   We will rally from the hillside, we'll gather from the plain,
   Shouting the battle-cry of freedom.

   Chorus:
   The Union forever, Hurrah, boys, hurrah!
   Down with the traitor and up with the star;
   While we rally round the flag, boys, rally once again,
   Shouting the battle-cry of freedom.

Omitting the repetitious theme "Shouting the battle-cry of freedom," which gave the new song its initial strength, the remaining stanzas contained these additional lines:

2. We are springing to the call of our brothers gone before,
   And we'll fill the vacant ranks with a million freemen more.
3. We will welcome to our numbers the loyal, true and brave,
   And although they may be poor, not a man shall be a slave.
4. So we're springing to the call from the East and from the West,
   And we'll hurl the rebel crew from the land we love the best.

31

Later, a "Battle Song" edition was prepared to supplement the original "Rallying Song" version, which contained these four stanzas, again omitting the repeated response as above:

1. We are marching to the field, boys, we're going to the fight,
   And we bear the glorious stars for the Union and the right.
2. We will meet the rebel host, boys, with fearless heart and true,
   And we'll show what Uncle Sam has for loyal men to do.
3. If we fall amid the fray, boys, we'll face them to the last,
   And our comrades brave shall hear us as they go rushing past.
4. Yes, for Liberty and Union we're springing to the fight,
   And the vict'ry shall be ours, for we're rising in our might.

Hardly had the ink dried on the original "Rallying Song" when Jule G. Lumbard, and his brother, the famous Lumbard singers of that day, entered Root's office with a request for an appropriate new war song for them to sing at a huge patriotic rally to be held almost immediately on the courthouse square opposite Root and Cady's office building. The composer taught them his new song and a few minutes later they sang it for the throngs across the street. When they reached the closing stanza, the assembled hundreds joined in on the responses and refrain, and from there it spread rapidly throughout all the northern states, its sudden popularity eliciting from the author-composer this remark, "It made me thankful that if I could not shoulder a musket in defense of my country, I could serve her in this way."

As soon as the song was published by Root and Cady, the composer sent the first printed copy to his wife back in North Reading. She taught it to one of her husband's former Normal School students, James R. Murray, who introduced it to the eastern section of the army almost at the same time that it was being sung by the soldiers in the western areas. Later some commanding officers ordered their divisions to sing this song when going into action, a tribute to the effect it had upon their morale. Twenty-five years later, in 1886, Mr. Root conducted a concert by Chicago's Apollo Club during which Mr. Jule G. Lumbard and the other singers sang, in the composer's honor, "The Battle Cry Of Freedom," making the rafters of the concert hall ring with their stirring rendition of one of Root's finest military songs.

During those memorable May days in 1861, Root found his place in the war and thereafter "when anything happened that could be voiced in a song, or when the heart of the Nation was moved by particular circumstances or conditions caused by the war," he wrote what he thought would then express the emotions of the soldiers and the civilians. During the Thanksgiving season of that first war year, 1861, he composed his music for H. S. Washburn's sentimental stanzas, "The Vacant Chair," which pictured a family gathering for the traditional feast, only to be conscious of the absence of the son who had fallen in the conflict and left "one vacant chair" to break the family circle on this otherwise festive occasion.

Two years later, in 1863, as he pictured the thoughts of a soldier on the eve of battle, he wrote the words and music of "Just Before The Battle, Mother":

1. Just before the battle, Mother, I am thinking most of you,
   While upon the field we're watching, With the enemy in
       view;
   Comrades brave around me lying, Filled with thoughts
       of home and God;
   For well we know that on the morrow, Some will sleep
       beneath the sod.

Chorus:

Farewell, Mother, you may never Press me to your heart
    again;
But, oh, you'll not forget me, Mother, If I'm numbered
    with the slain.
2. Oh, I long to see you, Mother, And the loving ones at
       home,
   But I'll never leave our banner, Till in honor I can come.
   Tell the traitors all around you That their cruel words we
       know

33

In every battle kill our soldiers, By the help they give the foe.

3. Hark! I hear the bugles sounding, 'Tis the signal for the fight;
   Now may God protect us, Mother, As He ever does the right.
   Hear "The Battle Cry Of Freedom," How it swells upon the air;
   Oh, yes, we'll rally round the standard, Or we'll perish nobly there.

In addition to his cantatas, popular songs and miscellaneous compositions (and Root published ninety-nine books or collections of music and seventy-eight separate songs during his lifetime), Root continued to make lasting contributions to sacred and Church music as well. His hymn tune "Varina" composed in 1856 for Rev. Isaac Watts' hymn on heaven, "There Is A Land Of Pure Delight," is still popular, while another stately tune, "Ellon," composed about 1871 for Mrs. Emily H. Miller's poem "I Love To Hear The Story," is found in many hymnals today, set to other stanzas, such as "The Wise May Bring Their Learning." In addition Root endeared himself to children by setting Rev. W. O. Cushing's sacred stanzas, "Jewels," to music, a song which is as popular with Sunday School scholars today as it was when Root composed it in 1856. The words and music of his "invitation hymn" "Why Do You Wait, Dear Brother?" are still a feature of many revivals in southern states. In 1864, when the shocking stories of returning prisoners revealed the terrible conditions of military prison camps, Root caught the mood of the moment and wrote a song for prisoners that contained the message of hope which was precisely what they, as well as their anxious loved ones back home, needed just then, "Tramp! Tramp! Tramp!"

1. In the prison cell I sit thinking Mother dear of you,
   And our bright and happy home so far away;
   And the tears they fill my eyes spite of all that I can do,
   Though I try to cheer my comrades and be gay.

Chorus:

Tramp, tramp, tramp, the boys are marching,
Cheer up, comrades, they will come;
And beneath the starry flag we shall breathe the air again
Of the free land in our own beloved home.

2. In the battle front we stood, when their fiercest charge
they made,
And they swept us off, a hundred men or more;
But before we reached their lines, they were beaten back
dismayed,
And we heard the cry of victory o'er and o'er.

3. So within the prison cell we are waiting for the day
That shall come to open wide the iron door;
And the hollow eyes grow bright and the poor heart almost
gay
As we think of seeing home and friends once more.

Years after the war was over, Rev. C. H. Woolston wrote
"sacred stanzas" to be sung to this particular tune, and today
many children sing the gospel hymn "Jesus Loves The Little
Children" who have never heard of "Tramp, Tramp, Tramp
The Boys Are Marching." Rev. W. O. Cushing did the same
thing with another one of Root's tunes, a piece of music he
composed for a secular song, "The Little Octoroon," penning
the stanzas of "Ring The Bells Of Heaven" as substitutes for
the original. College Glee Clubs still include in their reper-
toires George F. Root's composition "There's Music In The
Air," a little number he wrote one day in New York and
thought so little of that he stuck it away in a desk drawer,
taking it out only at the insistent request of the Mason
Brothers, who wanted something new for one edition of
their monthly journal "The Musical Review."

In the tragic Chicago fire of 1871, Root and Cady lost
everything, and closed up, but they reopened four years later,
in 1875, and their principal composer continued to write
for publication as prolifically as ever. In 1881, the University
of Chicago honored him with a Doctor of Music Degree, an
honor which he had been instrumental in persuading New

York University to confer upon Lowell Mason many years before.

In writing his autobiography during his seventieth year, Mr. Root, who was then universally respected, admired and loved as a "gentleman of the old school," said, "My wife and I would be glad to be permitted to see our golden wedding day which will be in 1895, and still more to look over into the twentieth century which will be five years later; but if that cannot be, we will be thankful for the pleasant life we have lived here and hope for a pleasanter and still more useful life hereafter." He lived only until their golden wedding anniversary month, dying at Bailey's Island, Maine, August 6, 1895.

No finer tribute could be paid the war songs of George F. Root than that spoken by a captured Confederate officer a few days after General Lee's surrender in April, 1865, who said to his captors, "Gentlemen, if we had had your songs, we'd have whipped you out of your boots! Who wouldn't have marched or fought with such songs? We had nothing, absolutely nothing, except a bastard 'Marseillaise' and 'The Bonny Blue Flag' and 'Dixie' which were nothing but jigs." Then, recalling an experience during The Seven Days Battles around Richmond when Lee lifted the siege of the Confederate capital, the southerner continued, "I shall never forget the first time I heard 'Rally Round The Flag.' It was a nasty night during the Seven Days fight, and it was raining. I was on picket, when, just before 'Taps,' some fellow on the other side struck up that song and others joined in the Chorus until it seemed to me the whole Yankee army was singing. A man with me said, 'Good heavens, Cap, what are those fellows made of anyway? Here we've licked them six days running and now on the eve of the seventh they're singing 'Rally Round The Flag!' I am not naturally superstitious, but I tell you that song sounded to me like the 'death knell' and my heart went down into my boots; and though I've tried to do my duty, it has been an uphill fight with me ever since." The victorious Yankee General added merely this one pertinent prophecy, which came true sooner than either soldier expected, "Well, the time may come when we can all sing 'The Star Spangled Banner' again."

MARYLAND, MY MARYLAND

James Ryder Randall, a direct descendant of Rene Leblanc who was immortalized in Longfellow's poem "Evangeline," was born in Baltimore, Maryland on New Years' Day, January 1, 1839, receiving his early scholastic training under a Baltimore Professor, Joseph H. Clarke. During his under-graduate years at nearby Georgetown College in Washington, D.C., he began to write poetry and even sold a few original stanzas to the Washington "Evening Star." After he received his Bachelor's degree, he spent a few months in extensive travel, visiting several Central and South American countries, returning to the United States in 1859 to clerk in a ship broker's office in New Orleans and then to become Professor of English at Poydras College, a Creole school whose campus was located on the Fausse Riviere, some thirty miles above Baton Rouge, Louisiana. The school had been named for a very interesting person, Julien De Lalande Poydras, a French-man by birth but an American by adoption, who was born in 1746 and died at the age of seventy-eight in 1824.

As a young and strikingly handsome man, Julien had fallen desperately in love with a strange young woman during the Mardi Gras, but since she was from a very poor home and knew that she could not bring her beloved a suitable dowry on their wedding day, she fled from New Orleans and never saw her fiancé again after that brief whirlwind courtship during the pre-Lenten festival. Poydras searched far and wide for his lost sweetheart but never found her. When he died he left in his will the sum of $30,000.00 each to Pointe Coupee (where the college was located) and West Baton

Rouge parishes in Louisiana, the income from which was to provide suitable dowries for the poor girls of the two parishes, since he suspected the reason behind the sudden, unexplained departure of his betrothed on the eve of their scheduled wedding day. The bulk of his fortune was set aside for the establishment of the school which bore his name. The foresight of the philanthropist was evident in another codicil of his will which provided for the freeing of all of his slaves at his death and the pensioning of all his slaves over sixty years of age. While his heirs were successful in preventing the carrying out of those measures, they were actually incorporated in the will of Julien Poydras. Had other southerners done the same thing, undoubtedly the war could have been averted if not avoided!

One of the poets whose works had intrigued the young English professor was James Clarence Mangan, an Irish author who had penned some stirring patriotic stanzas prior to his death in 1849. Randall often read aloud to his students these haunting and melancholy lines from Mangan's poignant pen:

> I see thee ever in my dreams, Karaman!
> Thy hundred hills, thy thousand streams, Karaman!
> As when thy gold-bright morning gleams,
> As when the deepening sunset seams
> With lines of light thy hills and streams, Karaman!
> So now thou loomest on my dreams, Karaman!

When the Civil War began, Randall reminded his students of the events which had led up to actual hostilities: February 4, 1861, the formation of the Confederate States of America; February 9, the election of Jefferson Davis as the first President; February 18, his inauguration in Montgomery, Alabama and February 22, his second inauguration at the new C.S.A. capital, Richmond, Virginia; April 12, the firing on Fort Sumter near Charleston, South Carolina; April 14, the surrender of the Fort to the Confederate forces; April 15, Lincoln's first call for troops (the President asked for 75,000 volunteers to increase the army to 150,000 men). Randall still considered himself a loyal citizen of the state of Maryland although he had been away from his native soil for many years. In his heart he felt that the state of Charles Carroll of Carrolton, a signer of the Declaration of Independence, and of John Eager Howard, a Revolutionary War soldier and hero and later Maryland's Governor and then a distinguished United States Senator, would do the right thing when the moment arrived, although he longed for her to cast her lot with the southern states instead of remaining loyal to the Union.

When Lincoln summoned troops from all over the north to come to the defense of Washington, among those who obeyed their Commander in Chief were the men of the Sixth Massachusetts Infantry who left Boston on Wednesday, April 16, 1861, for the beleagured capital. On Saturday, April 19, as they marched through Baltimore on the way to the Camden Street Station where they were to entrain immediately for Washington, some hot-headed, radical southern sympathizers opened fire on them, and in the melee that ensued, three soldiers and nine civilians lost their lives, while scores on both sides were wounded. When the news of that tragedy appeared in the columns of the New Orleans *Delta* a day or two later, one of his students brought a copy to Professor Randall, who was horrified as he read the account of that unfortunate occurrence. "It can't be possible," he said, "that in Baltimore, Maryland, Americans are actually killing other Americans." The thought of it inflamed his mind so he could think of nothing else for the rest of the day. That night his nerves were still so unstrung that he could not sleep. About midnight he got up from his bed, lit a candle, went to his desk, picked up his pen, dipped it in the inkwell and proceeded, almost involuntarily, to write some stanzas that had been burning inside of him. Thinking of the love which he held for his native state, and of the blood that flecked the streets of Baltimore and all the stark horror of that senseless strife, he penned his lines in the heat of patriotic fervor and in the peculiar meter of Mangan's "Karaman," since he had so recently read those unusual Poe-esque lines to one of his classes in English literature. Before he put down his pen that memorable night, nine separate stanzas had

39

flowed from his facile pen "not in cold blood but under what
may be called a conflagration of the senses, if not an inspiration of the intellect:"

1. The despot's heel is on thy shore, Maryland!
   His torch is at thy temple door, Maryland!
   Avenge the patriotic gore
   That flecked the streets of Baltimore,
   And be the battle-queen of yore, Maryland, my Maryland!
2. Hark to an exiled son's appeal, Maryland!
   My Mother State, to thee I kneel, Maryland!
   For life and death, for woe and weal,
   Thy peerless chivalry reveal,
   And gird thy beauteous limbs with steel, Maryland, my
   Maryland!
3. Thou wilt not cower in the dust, Maryland!
   Thy beaming sword shall never rust, Maryland!
   Remember Carroll's sacred trust,
   Remember Howard's warlike thrust,
   And all thy slumberers with the just, Maryland, my
   Maryland!
4. Come! 'tis the red dawn of the day, Maryland!
   Come with thy panoplied array, Maryland!
   With Ringgold's spirit for the fray,
   With Watson's blood at Monterey,
   With fearless Lowe and dashing May, Maryland, my
   Maryland!
5. Dear Mother, burst the tyrant's chain, Maryland!
   Virginia shall not call in vain, Maryland!
   She meets her sisters on the plain—
   "Sic Semper!" 'tis the proud refrain
   That baffles minions back again, Maryland, my Maryland!
6. Come! for thy shield is bright and strong, Maryland!
   Come! for thy dalliance does thee wrong, Maryland!
   Come to thine own heroic throng
   Stalking with liberty along,
   And chant thy dauntless slogan-song, Maryland, my Mary-
   land!
7. I see the blush upon thy cheek, Maryland!

For thou wast ever bravely meek, Maryland!
But lo! there surges forth a shriek
From hill to hill, from creek to creek,
Potomac calls to Chesapeake, Maryland, my Maryland!
8. Thou wilt not yield to vandal toll, Maryland!
Thou wilt not crook to his control, Maryland!
Better the fire upon thee roll,
Better the shot, the blade, the bowl,
Than crucifixion of thy soul, Maryland, my Maryland!
9. I hear the distant thunder hum, Maryland!
The Old Line's bugle, fife and drum, Maryland!
She is not dead, nor deaf, nor dumb;
Huzza! she spurns the Northern scum!
She breathes! She burns! She'll come, she'll come! Maryland, my Maryland!

The following day, Randall sat down beneath a large oak tree on the campus and made a copy of his new poem which he immediately sent to the New Orleans newspaper in which he had read the original dispatch, and it was printed in full in the Sunday *Delta* of April 26, 1861. The author said later, "No one was more surprised than I was at the widespread and instantaneous popularity of the lyric I had been so strangely stimulated to write." James Russell Lowell, poet, praised it as "the very best poem of the Civil War."

Among those who read and re-read the stirring stanzas during the weeks following their initial appearance in the New Orleans newspaper were two Baltimore sisters, Jennie and Hetty Cary. When the Baltimore City Glee Club scheduled a rehearsal in the Cary home one hot night in July, 1861, the sisters were looking for an appropriate new patriotic song to "liven up the practice session" when Hetty suggested she use the new poem "Maryland, my Maryland" which she had read in a recent local newspaper and clipped and saved for just such an occasion. When Jennie glanced at the stanzas, the only tune that flashed into her mind was "Lauriger Horatius," the tune of a college song which a young Yale student, Burton Harrison, had taught her recently. College students had written their Latin stanzas to fit the music of a German song "Tannenbaum, O Tannenbaum" ("Hemlock Tree, O Hemlock Tree" or "Christmas Tree, O Christmas Tree"), which was actually a folk tune from the Middle Ages. Anyway, fitting the new stanzas to the old tune, and repeating the name of her native state twice at the end of the first, second and last lines of each stanza, Jennie sang the new patriotic song for her guests that night with an effect that was described as "electric with excitement." Her enthusiasm was communicated to all who heard her and from that contagious moment on, "Maryland, my Maryland" became "The Marseillaise" of the Confederacy.

Barred by physical disabilities from enlisting in the Confederate army, Randall worked with several southern newspapers during the war years, particularly with the Augusta, Georgia "Chronicle." In the years that followed the conflict, he served as secretary to a Congressman and a Senator from Georgia, passing away in Augusta in his sixty-ninth year, on January 14, 1908.

Poydras College burned to the ground in 1881, and today the famous oak tree under which the poet-professor had copied his stanzas, now a well-known landmark, is all that remains. Although Maryland did not heed Randall's exhortation, but threw in her lot with the northern states, and while the author himself never again lived within the bounds of the state he loved so dearly, the song he was inspired to write became one of the best-known and most-sung of the tragic war years and is now considered the official state song of Maryland.

WE ARE COMING, FATHER ABRAHAM

President Abraham Lincoln's heirs can boast that more songs were written about him than any political statesman

42

in American history, for more than five-hundred separate compositions about The Great Emancipator came from the presses of the nation's music publishing houses during his terms of office and following his assassination at the hands of actor John Wilkes Booth. Some of them were nomination or presidential campaign songs while others were inspired by his emancipation proclamation of 1863. Nearly one-hundred were composed after his death, in the form of funeral marches and dirges or memorial hymns.

It is somewhat ironic that a peace-loving Quaker was the man who penned one of the most popular "Lincoln" songs of them all, and that it was a "call to arms" that led him to do it. The Quakers had been against human slavery as far back as 1688, so it was perfectly natural that the fourteen children of the Wilmington, Delaware, physician, Dr. William Gibbons and his wife, Rebecca Donaldson Gibbons, accepted the convictions of their distinguished and devout parents, and continued the fight against slavery with their same zeal, passion and sincerity. The physician-father, who had been the youngest of thirteen children himself, had been born in Philadelphia, August 10, 1781. After graduating from the medical college of the University of Pennsylvania in 1805, he had taken over the medical practice of Dr. John Vaughan in nearby Wilmington, Delaware, where he was to make his home for the next thirty-eight years, until his death on July 2, 1843. His wife also was a dedicated Quaker and was instrumental, after her husband's death, in founding the Wilmington Home for Aged Women. Dr. Gibbons, in addition to being a staunch abolitionist, was also a talented linguist, having a reading knowledge of five languages. In his spare time, he studied meteorology, edited a religious journal, "Berean," learned horticulture and campaigned against the reading of novels and the use of music in Church services, his negative "virtues" being in vivid contrast to his positive "virtues."

Two of their sons, Henry and William, became prominent physicians and distinguished botanists, while James Sloan Gibbons, the subject of this story, entered the business world with marked success. James' mother lived long enough to see slavery eradicated from American life at the close of the Civil War, and rejoiced that her son had a hand in its demise, for she lived to the age of eighty-one, passing away in 1869. At a time when no one else seemed to be concerned with the plight of the Negro slave in the United States, the Abolitionist Quakers of Delaware kept the fires of emancipation alive, and their labors were finally crowned with the success they merited.

Son James was born in Wilmington in 1810, and, following the completion of his education in a local Quaker (Friends) School, went back to his father's birthplace, Philadelphia, to become a dry goods merchant. On February 14, 1833, Valentine's Day, he married Abigail Hopper, the daughter of another Quaker who was also a wealthy philanthropist, little dreaming that she would one day be called "The Elizabeth Fry of America" for her achievements in the areas of prison reform and the emancipation of colored slaves.

In 1835, James and Abigail moved to New York City where he became such a well-known banker that he even wrote two "noteworthy" books on the subject, "The Banks of New York, Their Dealers, The Clearing House and The Panic of 1857" and "The Public Debt of The United States." Like his father before him, James had many other interests in addition to the profession by means of which he earned his daily bread. His interest in forest preservation led him to sponsor the movement that resulted in the observance of Arbor Day, while in their anti-slavery agitation, both husband and wife proved themselves so effective that they even out-Quakered the Quakers themselves. As early as 1842 they were disowned by the Quaker Meeting in New York City on account of their connection with the publication of the "National Anti-Slavery Standard," but Abigail's father, Isaac Tatem Hopper, came to their financial rescue on several occasions, although once James had to mortgage their home in order to keep the magazine going.

At the outbreak of hostilities, after Fort Sumter was fired upon, April 12, 1861, President Lincoln issued a call for 75,000 troops on April 15, 1861, sharing the conviction of many of his fellow countrymen that the war would be of brief duration. On May 3, he issued a proclamation calling enough men into active service to swell the rolls of the army to more than 150,000 and the navy to 25,000. But after the debacle at the First Battle of Manassas (Bull Run), in July, 1861, and the subsequent humiliating defeats of the Union armies in the Seven Days Battles, when General Robert E. Lee raised the siege of Richmond and pushed the invading forces far down the Virginia peninsula, Lincoln realized that it would take many more men and many more years before the south could be defeated and the Union preserved. Consequently, on July 1, 1862, he issued his historic call for 300,000 more men to serve for three years, wondering whether the country would "take to it" or not! (The first Union draft law, conscripting men into the armed forces, was not issued until March 3, 1863. In the Confederate States of America, the first draft law was passed April 16, 1862.) "Little Mac" General McClellan, who was begging for 50,000 more soldiers right away to reinforce his depleted forces, since he had lost 16,000 in the week of fighting outside the Confederate capital (as against 20,000 casualties for the men in gray) heard from his Commander in Chief. All Lincoln asked of him was to "be patient."

Among those who learned of this urgent appeal for more soldiers was Banker Gibbons, who read about it in the daily newspaper in his home on Lamartine Place in New York city. Later that evening as he listened to the tramp of marching feet on the street outside his home, he seemed to sense a strange martial atmosphere in the air, and, quite spontaneously, as the feet of the seemingly never-ending line of recruits marched continuously by, he found himself forming words and phrases, matching the call of the President to the response of the people, and soon he was writing down some original stanzas, in which he revealed his devotion to the Chief Executive by ascribing to him the filial appellation "Father Abraham":

1. We are coming, Father Abraham, three-hundred thousand more,

From Mississippi's winding streams and from New England's shore;
We leave our plows and workshops, our wives and children dear,
With hearts too full for utterance, with but a silent tear;
We dare not look behind us, but steadfastly before.
We are coming, Father Abraham, three-hundred thousand more.

2. If you look across the hilltops that meet the northern sky,
Long moving lines of rising dust your vision may descry;
And now the wind an instant tears the cloudly veil aside,
And floats aloft our spangled flag in glory and in pride;
And bayonets in the sunlight gleam, and bands brave music pour;
We are coming, Father Abraham, three-hundred thousand more.

3. If you look up our valleys where the growing harvests shine,
You may see our sturdy farmer boys fast forming color line;
And children from their mother's knee are pulling at the weeds,
And learning how to reap and sow against their country's needs;
And a farewell group stands weeping at every cottage door;
We are coming, Father Abraham, three-hundred thousand more.

4. You have called us and we're coming by Richmond's bloody tide,
To lay us down for freedom's sake, our brother's bones beside;
Or from foul treason's savage grasp to wrench the murderous blade,
And in the face of foreign foes its fragments to parade.
Six-hundred thousand loyal men and true have gone before—
We are coming, Father Abraham, three-hundred thousand more!

46

As soon as he had completed his poem, the fifty-two-year-old banker, who was too old to enter active military service, made a copy of his four verses and sent it to the New York "Evening Post." When the stanzas were published in the July 12, 1862 edition of that newspaper they were mistakenly attributed to one of the country's leading poets and abolitionists, William Cullen Bryant, who was at that time the editor of the journal, but a later edition carried a notice by Bryant to the effect that the poem was not his at all, but had come from the pen of James S. Gibbons. Set to music by different composers, it was an instantaneous success, its patriotic appeal coupled with its sentimental phrases and its swinging rhythm capturing the imagination of the war-weary people almost at once.

Tunes by such well known singers and composers as Hutchinson, Stephen Foster and Luther Orlando Emerson were quickly published and sold and once widely distributed throughout the states of the Union, it became one of the great favorites of the turbulent time.

That a Quaker should have written such a spirited marching song may seem incongruous but that he and his family should have suffered violence in a northern state because of their anti-slavery sentiments is even more so. During the destructive draft riots that raged in New York city from July 13 through 16, 1863, following and in protest against the enactment of the first Union draft law of the previous March 3, angry mobs broke into the Gibbons' home, sacked it, destroyed many valuable papers, burned priceless documents, and even endangered the lives of the banker and his family. The house was then daubed and defiled with coal tar, the crowds being angered because the ardent opponent of slavery had illumined it brightly on the occasion of Lincoln's issuance of his famous Emancipation Proclamation. The family survived this hardship, however, and after the war, they labored for prison reform as vigorously as they had for the other cause in previous decades.

To the union of James and Abigail Gibbons, six children were born, and the family remained loyal to the Quaker faith all the days of their lives. The financier-poet died in

New York City at the age of eighty-two, on October 17, 1892, while his wife, who was nine years his senior (she was born December 7, 1801) passed away three months later, on January 16, 1893, in her ninety-second year. One biographer concluded his account of James S. Gibbons' life and works with this statement, "With such a remarkable father, committed to freedom for Negro slaves; with a mother who also devoted her life to human betterment; with a wife and a father-in-law who supported every movement designed to crush slavery in the United States, and with a lifelong hostility to slavery—it is scarcely to be wondered that James Sloan Gibbons not only supported the War of 1861-65 as a necessary evil, but also contributed one of its famous marching songs, almost as popular in its day as 'John Brown's Body.' " History records, however, the strange fact that Lincoln's call for 300,000 volunteers, coupled with strong, stirring patriotic appeals by other civil and military leaders, in addition to promises of larger and larger cash bounties for all enlistees, and war songs by the dozen, brought in only 91,000 additional men, the need for more soldiers being taken care of finally in the passage of the first Union conscription law eight months later! And even then, most of the men on both sides hadn't the slightest idea what they were fighting for, but merely went about their duties because someone else over them in authority commanded them so to do. The tragedy of it all is that so much valuable human blood was shed for a cause that was hardly worth the cost of one human life, because political decisions are made and unmade by finite men while men are created by and in the image of the infinite God.

LORENA

The song sweetheart of the Second World War was Lily Marlene, while her First World War counterpart was known as the anonymous "Mademoiselle from Armentieres." The Spanish-American War did not last long enough to produce a symbolic female, but it is beyond question that the sweetheart of both the north and the south during the years of the Civil War was "Lorena." In fact, after the cessation of hostilities, some southern Generals blamed the loss of the war on that very song, affirming that "Confederates sang the 'cursed ballad,' grew homesick, deserted and thereby lost the war." Although, like Benjamin Hanby's Uncle Tom's Cabin of Song "Darling Nellie Gray," this ballad was published some years prior to the outbreak of the four-year conflict, it seemed to be just what the homesick, sentimental, heart-broken lads in blue and gray needed during their forced and prolonged absences from home and loved ones.

The story of Lorena began when a talented young clergyman, Rev. Henry De Lafayette Webster (1824-1896), accepted the pastoral oversight of the Universalist Church, then located on the corner of Underwood and Zane Streets in Zanesville, Ohio, in the 1840s. At that time Zanesville was a small town that lacked some of the cultural advantages that wealth, education and aristocracy usually afford. The community could boast of a famous heroine, however, for Betty Zane had so captured the admiration and imagination of her friends and fellow-townsmen by her one act of reckless bravery that they had later named their growing village in her honor. During an Indian attack on September 27, 1777, Betty had ignored the threats of the red men and had carried a cask of gunpowder in her apron to the besieged settlers who were then pinned down in a log hut by the severity and ferocity of the Indians. The attackers themselves were so shocked by her sudden heroic deed that they themselves held their "fire" until she was safely inside the beleaguered fortress. But, in later years, Betty was compelled to share her fame with another Zanesville maiden, Miss Ella Blocksom, because Ella was the girl who became the subject matter as well as the inspiration of the young Universalist minister's popular love song.

Ella was making her home with her sister and brother-in-law, Mr. and Mrs. Henry Blandy, in Prospect Place, Zanesville, when Webster came upon the scene, and it was with growing concern that the Blandys realized that a romance was blossoming between the two young people. While some townsfolk looked upon such a romance as "inevitable" or even "providential," that sentiment was not shared by the couple with whom Ella made her home, especially in view of the fact that the Blandys were numbered among the few "wealthy cultured aristocrats" of Zanesville, who kept drumming into Ella's unhearing ears the stark truth that Henry, on a poor preacher's salary, would never be able to provide her with the luxury to which she had become accustomed. So, just when other members of the local congregation thought that a wedding date had been set and would soon be publicly announced, Ella Blocksom received an "ultimatum" from her sister and brother-in-law, to the effect that "unless you terminate this unfortunate affair with that young preacher, you will be disinherited!" Yielding to their insistent pressure, Ella promised to break off her deepening friendship with Rev. Henry Webster at the earliest possible moment.

That fateful night, the young couple met for the last time, walking slowly to their familiar trysting-place on top of a hill overlooking the Ohio town, clasping the hands that so soon would be parted forever. Henry knew that if they ran away and married, he would have to give up the ministry, and that would create a great gulf between them that not even time would be able to bridge. As it was, he realized that once their unofficial engagement was broken, his ministry in Zanesville was at an end. As they returned to the Blandy's home later that evening, too heart-heavy to speak, yet praying for a miracle that they knew would never take place, Ella confessed that "duty had won over love." Webster shortly thereafter resigned his pulpit, packed up his belongings and went west in a futile effort to forget the one great love of his life by giving himself unreservedly to the service of the pioneers of the rapidly expanding frontier. Their engagement was more than likely terminated in May of 1849, but more than eight long years were to pass before he expressed his anguish and anxiety in the poem that brought him fame and renown.

During the months of their courtship doubtless Henry and Ella had spent many hours reading aloud some of the romantic poems of Edgar Allen Poe (1809-1894) whose writings were then all the rage, and they must have talked about the poet's lost love, Lenore, whom he immortalized in several of his finest literary compositions. All of those memories came crowding back into the heart and mind of the thirty-four year old clergyman when, late in the year 1856, he began to reduce his experience to poetry and write down the stanzas of his love song for posterity. Maybe the falling leaves of late September made him more conscious of his lost love than ever before, or possibly the happiness he read in the eyes of other young lovers caused him once again to remember the love-light that he had once seen in the eyes of his own betrothed. In order not to embarrass his former sweetheart back in Ohio, Henry created or adopted the name "Lorena," because, even after his poem was set to music and became the most popular love song of the day, those who knew Webster wondered if Ella Blocksom, whoever she may have married and wherever she may have been living, knew that she had been both the subject and inspiration of those six stanzas. Taking the letters of her name, "Ella," and coupling them with Poe's "lost Lenore," Henry came up with his new name, since Lorena, up to that particular time, was not used as a girl's name at all, and, until Webster fashioned it, does not appear in any other song or story up to that date. In that late September of 1857, the heart-broken preacher penned these autobiographical lines:

1. The years creep slowly by, Lorena; the snow is on the
     grass again;
   The sun's low down the sky, Lorena; the frost gleams
   where the flowers have been.
   But the heart throbs on as warmly now, as when the summer days were nigh;
   Oh! the sun can never dip so low, adown affection's cloud-
   less sky.
2. A hundred months have passed, Lorena, since last I held
     that hand in mine,

And felt that pulse beat fast, Lorena; though mine beat
faster far than thine.
A hundred months; 'twas flowery May, when up the hilly
slope we climbed,
To watch the dying of the day, and hear the distant church
bells chime.

3. We loved each other then, Lorena, more than we ever
dared to tell,
And what we might have been, Lorena, had but our lov-
ings prospered well.
But then 'tis past, the years are gone; I'll not call up their
shadowy forms;
I'll say of them, "Lost years, sleep on; sleep on, nor heed
life's pelting storms."

4. The story of the past, Lorena, alas! I care not to repeat;
The hopes that could not last, Lorena, they lived, but only
lived to cheat.
I would not cause e'en one regret, to rankle in your bosom
now;
For "if we try we may forget" were words of thine long
years ago.

5. Yes, these were words of thine, Lorena, they burn within
my memory yet;
They touched some tender chords, Lorena, which thrill
and tremble with regret.
'Twas not thy woman's heart that spoke; thy heart was
always true to me;
A duty stern and pressing broke the tie which linked my
soul with thee.

6. It matters little now, Lorena; the past is in the eternal past;
Our heads will soon lie low, Lorena; life's tide is ebbing
out so fast.
There is a future! Oh, thank God! Of life this is so small a
part!
'Tis dust to dust beneath the sod; but there, up there,
'tis heart to heart.

Shortly after Henry Webster wrote these pathetic lines, he
chanced to run into a popular musician and composer, Joseph

Philbrick Webster (1819-1875) who was no relation even though they both had the same last name. He happened to mention the poem he had recently written, and, at the musical Webster's insistence, he let him read it. Joseph then persuaded Henry to let him set the words to music, to which Henry agreed. J. P. Webster, a native of Manchester, New Hampshire, where he had been born March 22, 1819, had lived in Boston for many years before moving west, holding membership in such well known musical organizations as the Handel and Haydn Society. He had composed a popular cantata on "The Beatitudes" as well as a wide variety of other secular and sacred music, so when he made his request of Henry Webster, Joseph was no novice in the field. He was also a talented violinist as well as a vocalist, and, for some years prior to the Civil War, had toured the northern states with a professional quartet, giving concerts and performances in many towns and cities. He wrote his hauntingly beautiful melody for "Lorena" a few weeks later, and a comparison with other compositions of the day shows that Webster's lovely music stands head and shoulders above most of the sentimental songs that other composers were turning out with rather montonous regularity. The same melody is used for the first and second lines of Henry's poem, while the third line moves to a relative minor key which adds to the plaintiveness of the music. The last line repeats the principal theme once more and then is itself repeated in a brief climax of four more measures. After writing down his melody and broken chord accompaniment, J. P. Webster sent the new song to a Chicago publisher who immediately recognized its worth and brought it out late that next year, 1857. The fame of "Lorena" spread rapidly on its wings of song, and by 1861 it was being published in Nashville and Memphis and becoming the favorite of the Confederate soldiers as well as the Yankees shortly thereafter.

On Thursday, September 1, 1864, the day that Atlanta was ordered evacuated by General John B. Hood before the arrival of superior forces under General William T. Sherman, the weary, war-worn Confederate soldiers trudged down McDonough Road, which was Hood's chief escape route, and, for many years thereafter, Georgians recalled the way the tired defenders sang "Lorena" as they turned their backs upon the devastated city and marched agonizingly south.

Tradition has it that "Lorena" did marry some years after breaking her engagement with the young clergyman, and that her husband, a member of the Home Guards during the War who was severely wounded in action, became a successful attorney in Ironton, Lawrence County, Ohio, rising to such prominence that he was appointed one of the five members of the Supreme Court Commission of the state, his wife being a faithful helpmate to him and sharing his high honors with "becoming dignity." After the Justice's death in 1887, she is supposed to have returned to the scenes of her childhood, spending her last years practically alone, since all of her close friends and relatives had preceded her in death.

As for Rev. Mr. Webster, he finally settled down in Wisconsin, gaining quite a reputation for himself as a writer, poet and journalist. When, after the passing of many more years, he heard no word whatsoever from his former fiancée, he wrote what he called a sequel to "Lorena," in which he spoke of himself as "Paul Vane." Published as "Paul Vane or Lorena's Reply," this poem was also set to music by Joseph P. Webster, and copyrighted again as late as 1900. For sometime it shared honors with the original in the affections of the people, but not for long, because its four stanzas somehow failed to touch the heart strings as had the preacher-poet's earlier success:

1. The years are creeping slowly by, dear Paul; the winters come and go.
   The wind sweeps past with mournful cry, dear Paul, and pelt my face with snow.
   But there's no snow upon the heart, dear Paul; 'tis summer always there;
   Those early loves throw sunshine over all, and sweeten memories care.
2. I thought it easy to forget, dear Paul; life glowed with youthful hope;
   The glorious future gleaméd yet, dear Paul, and bade us clamber up.

The frowning said, "It must not, cannot be; break now the hopeless bands."

And Paul, you know how well that bitter day, I bent to their commands.

3. I've kept you ever in my heart, dear Paul, through years of good and ill;

Our souls could not be torn apart, dear Paul; they're bound together still.

I never knew how dear you were to me, till I was left alone;

I thought my poor heart would break that day they told me you were gone.

4. Perhaps we'll never, never meet, dear Paul, upon this earth again;

But there, where happy angels greet, dear Paul, you'll meet Lorena there.

Together ever up the shining way, we'll press with hoping heart,

Together through the bright eternal day, and never more to part.

Composer J. P. Webster settled down in Elkhorn, Wisconsin, where, one afternoon in the late fall of 1867, he ran into his friend, the proprietor, Samuel Fillmore Bennett (1836-1898) in the local drugstore. When Bennett noticed that the musician was somewhat sad and morose, he "snapped him out of it" by taking one of Webster's own expressions, "Everything will be all right in the bye and bye" and writing, almost spontaneously, the stanzas of the gospel song "The Sweet Bye and Bye," encouraging Webster to set it to music immediately. Taking out his violin, the moody composer did just that, the new song being published the very next year, 1868, in Webster's collection of Sunday School songs, "The Signet Ring." Maybe the composer, as he set Bennett's words to music that day, was thinking of Lorena and Paul Vane, and wondering if they, too, would "in the sweet bye and bye" meet on that beautiful shore!

MARCHING THROUGH GEORGIA

One day during the late summer of 1861, a rather solemn and quiet young man entered the reception room of the Chicago music publishing firm of Root and Cady and asked an employee there to examine the manuscript of a new song he had just recently written. The worker sent him upstairs to the office of George F. Root, the well-known music teacher, who was then, at the age of forty, one of the country's leading composers of popular and semi-classic music. The publishing company was only three years old that memorable afternoon, having been founded in 1858 by George's brother E. T. Root and C. T. Cady, who had studied under George when Cady was a student at Union Theological seminary in New York City several years earlier. When the unknown twenty-eight year old musician knocked at Root's office door a few moments later, the older man said, "Come in."

The door opened and a poorly-clad composer stood there, manuscript in hand, mumbling something about having written and composed a new song that he wanted some publisher to look over and consider. When he took the song and began to examine it carefully, with the well-trained eye and ear of a successful and popular publisher, George F. Root realized almost immediately that he had stumbled upon something out of the ordinary. He looked at the music and then at the man in utter astonishment, because the song was "elegantly written out" and "full of bright good sense and comical situations in its darkey dialect, the words fitting the melody almost as aptly and neatly as Gilbert fits Sullivan, the melody decidely good and taking, the whole exactly suited to the times."

What Root was holding in his hand that afternoon was the original manuscript of the popular Civil War song, "King-

dom Coming," by the poet and composer Henry Clay Work
(1832-1884), the stanzas of which contained these lines:

1. Say, darkeys, hab you seen de massa wid de muffstas on his
     face,
   Go long de road sometime dis mornin' like he gwine to
     leab de place?
   He seen a smoke way up de ribber whar de Linkum gun-
     boats lay,
   He took his hat an' lef' berry sudden An' I spec he's run
     away.

   Chorus:

   De massa run, ha! ha! de darkeys stay, ho! ho!
   It mus' be now de kingdom comin' an de year ob Jubilo!
2. De darkeys feel so lonesome, libing in de log-house on de
     lawn,
   Dey move dar tings to massa's parlor for to keep it while
     he's gone.
   Dar's wine an' cider in de kitchen an' de darkeys dey'll hab
     some;
   I spose dey'll all be confiscated when de Linkum sojers
     come.
3. De oberseer he make us trouble, An' he dribe us round a
     spell;
   We lock him up in de smoke-house cellar wid de key trown
     in de well.
   De whip is lost, de han' cuff broken but de massa'll hab
     his pay;
   He's ole enough, big enough, ought to know better dan
     to went an' run away.

   Root looked up and asked, "Did you write this, words and
music?"
   The young man answered gently, "Yes."
   The publisher continued, "What is your business, if I
may inquire?"
   "I am a printer," Work replied.
   "Would you rather write music than set type?" Root asked,
realizing that he had a rare find indeed in the musical and

57

poetic skills of this comparatively unknown standing before him, to which Work answered, "Yes."

Root concluded the interview with this observation, "Well, if this is a specimen of what you can do, I think you may give up the printing business." A contract was then drawn up and signed and Work became a song writer in the employ of Root and Cady as of that date.

Before that time, about the only money his song writing had ever brought him was the sum of $25 which he received when he sold his first song "We're Coming, Sister Mary" to Christy's Minstrels, but little did the young printer dream when he affixed his name to that contract that afternoon that one of his future songs, "Grandfather's Clock," would sell more than eight-hundred thousand copies and earn him in a few years more than $4,000 in royalties. When his new employer inquired into his background, he learned that Henry Clay Work had been born in Middletown, Connecticut, October 1, 1832, the son of Alanson and Aurelia Work. Alanson had moved his family to Quincy, Illinois, when the lad was only three years of age, in order to aid run-away slaves, making his home a station on the "underground railroad" that assisted over four-thousand escaped slaves on their way to freedom farther north in Canada. His efforts brought him into conflict with the local authorities, however, and, after a period of imprisonment for his abolition sentiments and activities, he returned to Middletown with his family in 1845. Henry was given a common school education, after which he was apprenticed to a local printer, Elihu Greer, and taught the trade he was practicing when he began to write his own songs some years later. When he discovered an old melodeon in a room over top of Greer's print shop, he soon became a self-taught musician, studying harmony in his spare time, and began playing and singing his own original songs whenever he could gather a sympathetic audience. He moved to Chicago in 1854, and worked there for seven years before he got up nerve enough to show one of his manuscripts to the leading music publisher in the Windy City. It was during his stay in Chicago that Work married, but, after the sudden death of two of their three children, his wife suffered a mental breakdown, preceding her husband in death by about a year, being buried in the Spring Grove Cemetery, Hartford, Connecticut, in 1883.

Work's association with Root and Cady was a mutually beneficial one, because they needed his songs and he needed their publishing and promoting. Two years after he began his connection with the new firm, Work published a "sequel" to "Kingdom Coming" which he entitled "Babylon Is Fallen." In the same vein that characterized his earlier success, and in a similar dialect to a catchy tune, he wrote:

1. Don't you see de black clouds risin' ober yonder,
   Whar de massa's ole plantation am?
   Never you be frightened, dem is only darkeys,
   Come to jine an' fight for Uncle Sam.

   Chorus:

   Look out dar, now! We's gwine to shoot, Look out dar,
      don' you understand?
   Babylon is fallen! Babylon is fallen! And we's gwine to
      occupy de land.
2. Don't you see de lightnin' flashin' in de canebrake,
   Like as if we's gwine to hab a storm?
   No! you is mistaken, 'tis de darkeys bay'nets,
   And de buttons on dar uniform.
3. Way up in de cornfield, whar you hear de tunder,
   Dat is our ole forty-pounder gun;
   Where de shells are missin', den we load wid punkins,
   All de same to make de cowards run.
4. Massa was de Kernel in de rebel army,
   Ebber since he went an' run away;
   But his lubly darkeys, dey has been a watchin'
   An' dey take him pris'ner tudder day.
5. We will be de massa, he will be de servant,
   Try him how he like it for a spell;
   So we crack de Butt'nuts, so we take de Kernel,
   So de cannon carry back de shell.

In 1864, Work revealed that he was as strong a prohibitionist as he was an abolitionist, for it was during that year that he wrote the popular temperance song that was to be featured with the play "Ten Nights In A Barroom" for the next eight decades:

> Father, dear father, come home with me now, The clock in the steeple strikes one;
> You said you were coming right home from the shop As soon as your day's work was done.

There then followed such other song successes as "Wake, Nicodemus," "Columbia's Guardian Angel," "God Save The Nation," "Little Major," "Corporal Schnapps" and the tearjerking "Brave Boys Are They":

> Heavily falls the rain, Wild are the breezes tonight;
> But 'neath the roof, the hours as they fly, Are happy and calm and bright.
> Gathering round our fireside, Though it be summer time,
> We sit and talk of brothers abroad, Forgetting the midnight chime.

Chorus:

> Brave boys are they! Gone at their country's call,
> And yet we cannot forget, That many brave boys must fall.

Early in 1864 when "Crusader Work believed the people wanted a song lifting Lincoln alongside the one American historic character whose fame had a whited sanctity beyond challenge or murmur," he dashed off the stanzas and tune of a new one entitled "Washington and Lincoln." Although his lines were criticized in the press as being everything bad from "flamboyant" to "flapdoodle," the people "ate them up" and soon were singing all over the northern states:

> Down through the ages an anthem shall go, Bearing the honors we gladly bestow;
> Till every nation and language shall know The story of Washington and Lincoln.

Like his employer, George F. Root (1820-1895), Henry Clay Work "had a public and wrote for them what he felt they wanted, and rarely guessed wrong." Even the soldiers approved of his pathetic lines and sang, as did their loved ones back home, the three stanzas of "Grafted Into The Army":

1. Our Jimmy has gone for to live in a tent,
They have grafted him into the army;
He finally puckered up courage and went,
When they grafted him into the army.
I told them the child was too young, alas!
At the Captain's fore-quarters they said he would pass,
They'd train him up well in the infantry class,
So they grafted him into the army.

Chorus:

Oh, Jimmy, farewell! Your brothers fell, way down in
Alabamy;
I thought they would spare a lone widder's heir,
But they grafted him into the army.

While Work, who never shouldered a musket or presented arms and could hardly distinguish one military bugle call from another, continued to turn out his popular war songs like proverbial 'hot cakes,' he reached the zenith of his powers late in 1864 and early in 1865 when he versified Sherman's march from Atlanta to the sea in what became one of the most popular songs of the entire period. Everyone, however, did not concur with the people's appraisal of the song or with the sentiments expressed therein, for the great General himself is said to have remarked confidentially to a friend some years after the cessation of hostilities, "If I had thought when I made that march that it would have inspired any one to compose the piece, I would have marched around the state."

General William Tecumseh Sherman (1820-1891) had commanded a brigade at the First Battle of Manassas (Bull Run) in July, 1861, and had later been elevated to the post of Brigadier General of Volunteers, assuming command of the Department of Kentucky. In 1862 he fought with Grant at Shiloh and the following year, as a Major General and Corps

Commander, participated in the siege and capture of Vicksburg, later leading the forces that relieved the besieged Union Army at Chattanooga. When President Lincoln appointed General U. S. Grant as Lieutenant General of all the Federal armies early in 1864, Sherman succeeded him as Commander of the Division of Mississippi and later that same year conceived of his dramatic and destructive "march to the sea" which, with its scorched earth policy, wiped out the south's last economic resources, for the soldiers under his command obeyed literally Sherman's Special Field Order Number 120, "The army will forage liberally on the country during the march." With three armies totalling about one-hundred thousand men, he took Atlanta, later taking two armies, numbering about sixty-three thousand soldiers, for the completion of his daring campaign, which began on November 15, 1864, and ended with the capture of Savannah twenty-five days later, December 10, 1864.

Just prior to the start of this march to the sea, when Sherman's huge army lay near Atlanta, there occurred an event which inspired the writing of what became one of the most stirring sacred songs of the next fifty years. General Hood, in a carefully prepared movement, passed Sherman's right flank, and gained his rear, commencing then the destruction of the railroad leading north in order to trap the Federals farther south. The Confederates burned blockhouses and captured numerous garrisons en route, while Sherman put his army in rapid pursuit of Hood in order to save the supplies piled up at Allatoona Pass. General J. M. Corse of Illinois, the twenty-eight-year-old commander, and his second in command, Colonel Tourtelotte, had only fifteen-hundred men with which to protect a million and a half rations for Sherman's forces, and it was essential that they hold the pass and the approaches thereto until the main body of the Federals could come to their defense and route Hood's men. The Confederate commander detached General French and six-thousand soldiers to take Corse's position, and they immediately surrounded the northern General and demanded his surrender, which was curtly refused. When fighting began, Corse and his men were driven into a small fort on top of the hill. Just when it seemed that all was lost that October 5, 1864, an officer, looking through his telescope for promised reinforcements, caught sight of a signal flag on top of Kenesaw Mountain some fifteen miles away. He answered the signal and immediately received this message, "Hold the fort, I am coming. W. T. Sherman." The signal flags, designed for the army by a medical officer, Albert J. Myer (after whom Fort Myer was named) who received his inspiration from the spear signals of the New Mexico Indians, did the trick. Although furious fighting continued and murderous assaults against the position were attempted by the Confederates time and time again, thrice-wounded Corse and his men held out until Sherman's advance guard compelled General French to call off his attackers and retreat to safety.

When Major Whittle told this story at a Sunday School convention in Rockford, Illinois, in May, 1870, Philip Bliss, the popular thirty-two-year-old song-leader and composer, was present. The very next day he spiritualized Sherman's message and introduced his new gospel song at a YMCA gathering in Chicago. Soon those present were joining in the moving strains of the new song, reading the words from a blackboard on which Bliss had just written them:

1. Ho! my comrades, see the signal, Waving in the sky!
   Reinforcements now appearing, Victory is nigh.

   Chorus:

   "Hold the fort, for I am coming," Jesus signals still;
   Wave the answer back to heaven, "By Thy grace, we will!"
2. See the mighty host advancing, Satan leading on;
   Mighty men around us falling, Courage almost gone.
3. See the glorious banner waving, Hear the bugle blow;
   In our Leader's Name we'll triumph Over every foe.
4. Fierce and long the battle rages, But our Help is near;
   Onward comes our Great Commander; Cheer, my comrades, Cheer!

Philip P. Bliss (1838-1876) wrote many fine gospel songs before his untimely death in a tragic railroad accident at

Ashtabula, Ohio at the age of thirty-eight, and such favorites as "Let The Lower Lights Be Burning" and "I Am So Glad That Jesus Loves Me" will continue to be sung for many years. But while the composer told his musical friend Ira D. Sankey that he hoped he would not be remembered only as the author of that particular song since he believed he had written many better ones, on a monument to his memory in Rome, Pennsylvania, are these words: P. P. Bliss, Author of "Hold The Fort." Sankey later directed many of his choirs with a baton made from a piece of wood taken from the very tree atop Kenesaw Mountain from which Sherman's message of encouragement had been signalled to Corse's beleaguered forces. But Henry Clay Work was inspired to write an entirely different type of song when he read of Sherman's victorious feat, and although the war was soon to end within a few bloody months, his song became the favorite of the northern states and before long they were singing together:

1. Bring the good old bugle boys, We'll sing another song,
   Sing it with a spirit that will start the world along;
   Sing it as we used to sing it, fifty-thousand strong,
   While we were marching through Georgia.

   Chorus:

   Hurrah! Hurrah! we bring the Jubilee!
   Hurrah! Hurrah! The flag that makes you free!
   So we sang the chorus from Atlanta to the sea,
   While we were marching through Georgia.
2. How the darkies shouted when they heard the joyful
      sound!
   How the turkeys gobbled which our commissary found!
   How the sweet potatoes even started from the ground,
   While we were marching through Georgia.
3. Yes, and there were Union men who wept with joyful
      tears
   When they saw the honored flag they had not seen for
      years;
   Hardly could they be restrained from breaking forth in
      cheers,

64

While we were marching through Georgia.
4. "Sherman's dashing Yankee boys will never reach the
   coast!"
   So the saucy rebels said, and 'twas a handsome boast;
   Had they not forgot, alas, to reckon with the host,
   While we were marching through Georgia.
5. So we made a thoroughfare for Freedom and her train,
   Sixty miles in latitude, three-hundred to the main;
   Treason fled before us for resistance was in vain,
   While we were marching through Georgia.

After the fall of Savannah, Sherman marched through the
Carolinas to attempt to effect an eventual union with Grant
in Virginia. He received the surrender of General Joseph E.
Johnston on April 26, 1865, just seventeen days after General
Lee had surrendered the Army Of Northern Virginia to his
adversary at Appomattox Court House, Virginia, April 9,
1865, and these two northern victories and southern defeats
marked the virtual cessation of Civil War hostilities, and the
final end of the four-year conflict. Sherman's "War is hell"
speech was delivered on June 19, 1879, by which time he was
as well qualified from personal experience to make such an
observation as any man in the country.

When Work equated the freeing of the slaves with the
Old Testament Year of Jubilee, he voiced an opinion or
conviction that was shared by a great many northern writers,
lecturers, preachers, soldiers and song-writers, and, whether
pronounced correctly "Jubilee" or mis-pronounced "Jubilo,"
came, more than likely, from the early camp-meeting hymns
in which the people had heralded the coming of the year of
Jubilee in such stanzas as this one, written and published in
1750 by Rev. Charles Wesley (1707-1788) co-founder of the
Methodist Church and one of the outstanding hymn writers
of Christian history:

Blow ye the trumpet, blow! The gladly solemn sound,
Let all the nations know, To earth's remotest bound.
The year of Jubilee is come! The year of Jubilee is come!
Return, ye ransomed sinners, home.

In this hymn, Wesley Christianized the ancient Hebrew law found in Leviticus 25:8-13, in which each fiftieth year was to be observed as "A Year of Jubilee," when the trumpet shall sound and they shall "proclaim liberty throughout the land unto all the inhabitants thereof" (the phrase inscribed on the Liberty Bell), and in which "ye shall return every man unto his possession and ye shall return every man unto his family," which to the oppressed slave meant a return to freedom!

It is not therefore surprising that this theme crept into their songs and hymns, and became an obsession with those who were not yet politically or economically emancipated! Whether the oppressed slaves in the south were any better prepared to exercise their freedom or had any more capacity to appreciate it than the children of Israel when they were granted their freedom under Moses after four-hundred years of slavery in Egypt is a problem with which historians will continue to cope for generations to come! But Work's publisher, George F. Root, himself the author and composer of some of the Civil War's most popular songs, attributed part of the success of "Marching Through Georgia" to the fact that it was a retrospective song, "a glorious remembrance on coming out triumphantly," while the majority of his own songs, Root admitted, were for "exciting patriotic feeling on going into the war or battle." For that reason, as well as because of "the intrinsic merit of its words and music," this song of Work, who was a "slow and painstaking writer, spending from one to three weeks on a song, which, when completed, resembled a piece of fine mosaic, especially in the fitting of words to music," "Marching Through Georgia," became as much a favorite at gatherings of soldiers, veterans and civilians after the war as it had been during the conflict and when Mr. Root wrote his autobiography in 1890, he confessed that it was being played and sung at that time more than any other song of the war, including his own! The royalties he received from these popular ballads enabled Work to take a European trip in 1865.

Following the terrible Chicago fire of 1871, Root and Cady went broke, since all the plates of all their publications

66

were destroyed in the flames that consumed the greater part of the city. Work then moved to Philadelphia and on to Vineland, New Jersey, where he lost a small fortune in real estate speculation, but when his publishers re-established their firm in 1875, he returned to Chicago and made more money than ever before, because it was during this time that he wrote "Grandfather's Clock," which, of his seventy-three published songs, is regarded as the finest and best. Its words and music continue to be favorites of each succeeding generation, as they sing, to the composer's lilting music, his nostalgic lines:

1. My grandfather's clock was too large for the shelf
   So it stood ninety years on the floor;
   It was taller by half than the old man himself
   Though it weighed not a penny-weight more.
   It was bought on the morn of the day that he was born,
   And was always his treasure and pride;
   But it stopped short, never to go again,
   When the old man died.

   Chorus:

   Ninety years without slumbering (tick, tock, tick, tock);
   His life seconds numbering (tick, tock, tick, tock);
   But it stopped short, never to go again,
   When the old man died.

Nine years after he returned to the employ of Root and Cady, Henry Clay Work travelled east to visit his mother in Hartford, Connecticut, and there he died, June 8, 1884, at the age of fifty-two, being buried beside his wife in Spring Grove Cemetery. His songs, many of which were written during the dark and gloomy days of the War of 1861-1865, did a great deal to give an aura of "sanctity and holiness" to those reluctant conscripts engaged in fratricidal strife, and to strengthen them to endure the sufferings which war always brings in its wake and to face the hardships and privations it constantly demands. Fortunately, he turned his talents in other directions when the war was over and revealed a genius that would otherwise have been hidden and a spark of senti-

67

ment that his war songs failed to uncover, and, undoubtedly, long after Sherman's march to the sea has been forgotten, "Grandfather's Clock" will continue to be sung, and the name and music of Henry Clay Work will be perpetuated thereby.

PRESIDENT ABRAHAM LINCOLN'S
FAVORITE HYMN

Although a snow storm inspired the writing of Lincoln's favorite sacred song, and a meeting of the United States Christian Commission (Chaplains Corps) in the Hall of the House of Representatives in Washington, D.C. popularized it, its success came as no surprise to the author, for when she finished writing down her six stanzas that winter afternoon in 1860, she "had a presentiment that it had wings and would fly into sorrowful hearts, uplifting and strengthening them." How right she was in her prophecy she did not know at that moment, and had she realized that the labors of two others were to be involved in its widespread ministry, possibly she would have tempered her predictions with regard to its future. But when Sidney M. Grannis and Philip Phillips got through with it, there was hardly a Christian in the English-speaking world who was not familiar with its ringing message of hope and good cheer.

The poet who had had that strange premonition that snowy afternoon was thirty-five-year-old Ellen Huntington Gates, wife of Isaac E. Gates, and sister of the financial wizard, Collis P. Huntington. She was born in Torrington, Connecticut in 1835, but for many years had made her home in New York City and later in Elizabeth, New Jersey. That particular afternoon she had planned to go out and her plans did not make any allowances for an unexpectedly heavy snow storm. But the weather man refused to cooperate and the snow came down in a blinding fury, blocking sidewalks and snarling traffic and generally upsetting Mrs. Gates' plans along with those of several million other New Yorkers. Her initial resentment soon melted, however, and, sitting by the window and looking outside, she began to muse with her better self, and soon found herself thinking, "If I cannot go out, then I can stay in," and while that was by no means a startlingly original or profound observation, it led her to add, "And if I cannot do something big, I can be content with doing something small. For example, if I cannot cross the ocean, I can help those who launch the ships that do, and if I cannot fight like Napoleon or Lord Nelson, I can bind up the soldier's and sailor's wounds like Florence Nightingale; and if I cannot gather up the grain in the fields of Boaz, I can glean among the left-overs like Ruth." As one new thought followed rapidly upon the wings of another, soon, instead of spending the afternoon in idle day-dreaming or neurotic self-pity, Ellen Gates began to write down her ideas in poetic form as they crowded into her fertile, imaginative mind. Even though she jotted her couplets down quite quickly, realizing that the entire poem was "such a simple little thing," that strange presentiment kept her from tearing up the piece of paper and throwing it into the fireplace. Although some of her lines have been altered and some phrases recast and edited in the intervening century, Mrs. Gates' original six stanzas contained these "simple but immortal" words, under the title "Your Mission":

1. If you cannot on the ocean
   Sail among the swiftest fleet,
   Rocking on the highest billows,
   Laughing at the storms you meet;
   You can stand among the sailors
   Anchored yet within the bay;
   You can lend a hand to help them
   As they launch their boats away.
2. If you are too weak to journey
   Up the mountain steep and high,
   You can stand within the valley

69

While the multitudes go by;
You can chant in happy measure,
As they slowly pass along;
Though they may forget the singer,
They will not forget the song.

3. If you have not gold and silver
Ever ready to command;
If you cannot towards the needy
Reach an ever open hand;
You can visit the afflicted,
O'er the erring you can weep;
You can be a true disciple
Sitting at the Saviour's feet.

4. If you cannot in the conflict
Prove yourself a soldier true;
If, where fire and smoke are thickest,
There's no work for you to do;
When the battlefield is silent,
You can go with careful tread;
You can bear away the wounded,
You can cover up the dead.

5. If you cannot in the harvest
Garner up the richest sheaves,
Many a grain both ripe and golden
Will the careless reapers leave;
Go and glean among the briars
Growing rank against the wall;
For it may be that their shadow
Hides the heaviest wheat of all.

6. Do not, then, stand idly waiting,
For some greater work to do;
Fortune is a lazy goddess,
She will never come to you.
Go and toil in any vineyard,
Do not fear to do or dare;
If you want a field of labor,
You can find it anywhere.

Following their initial publication, it did not take Sidney M. Grannis very long to set these stanzas to music, al-

70

though they could have been sung much more effectively to several standard 8.7.8.7.D. hymn tunes, such as "Autumn," "Nettleton" or "Hyfrydol." But, just as some singers can ruin a splendid piece of music by making it sound worse than it really is, others have the wonderful gift of being able to interpret a second-rate, mediocre composition so effectively that it sounds much better than it actually is, and that is what happened with Grannis' tune.

The eighth and sixteenth notes in his melody tend to destroy the smoothness needed in an impressive sacred solo, and the composer's mania for repeating the last phrase of each stanza as an intended "dramatic climax" (he did the very same thing in his musical setting of Caroline Mason's sentimental poem "Do They Miss Me At Home?") is anti-climactic and possibly was one of the factors that led Lincoln's biographer, Carl Sandburg, to speak of the tune as "banal and second-rate." Strangely enough, though, the music so appealed to Ira D. Sankey that when he looked in a newspaper one day and found Rev. Daniel March's hymn-poem "Hark! The Voice Of Jesus Calling" which the Congregational clergyman wrote in Philadelphia in October, 1868, and realized that it was penned in the same poetic meter as Mrs. Gates' "Your Mission," he appropriated Mr. Grannis' tune and set it to March's six stanzas, including the hymn as Number 640 in the 1894 edition of "Gospel Hymns, Numbers 1 to 6 Complete," while even as late as 1922, the Hope Publishing Company of Chicago included Gates and Grannis as Hymn 99 in the collection entitled "Hymns Of Praise." (March's hymn has been sometimes confused with Mrs. Gates' stanzas because of the similarity of expression common to both. While Mrs. Gates wrote, "If you cannot *on* the ocean Sail among the swiftest fleet," Dr. March wrote, eight years later, "If you cannot *cross* the ocean And the heathen lands explore.")

What put "Your Mission" over, however, was the singing of a remarkable man, Philip Phillips (1834-1895). Farm-born and musically self-educated, this talented New Yorker had the nerve to peddle his own original songs from house to house by the time he was twenty-one, and soon began conducting singing-schools as well. When he saved enough money to go into business for himself, he opened a music store and publishing house in Fredonia, New York, travelling far and wide as an evangelistic singer on the side. His trips eventually took him on what he called "A Song Pilgrimage Around The World," and, before his death at sixty-one, he could boast that he had given more than three-thousand song services to the glory of God.

Early in 1865, Phillips was invited to sing at the meeting of the New Jersey Conference of The Methodist Church being held in the city of Trenton. Although he was almost a total stranger to most of the two-thousand ministers and lay-men in attendance, he began his program by sitting at his little organ and playing and singing "Your Mission." By the time he reached the fifth verse, "every eye was a fountain of tears," while the Governor of the State and other elected officials present "wept like children." At the conclusion of the solo, and the singing of the closing lines:

If you want a field of labor, You can find it anywhere,

Bishop Ames brought the congregation back to reality by solemnly saying, "I hope the brethren will remember that when they get their appointments!"

A few days later, in February, 1865, Phillips, then a better-known evangelistic singer, was invited to be present at the final anniversary meeting of the "United States Christian Commission" to be held in the Hall of the House of Representatives in the capitol building in Washington, D.C. A picture drawn by one who attended that memorable gathering reveals that every seat on the floor and in the balcony was filled, while many extra chairs were placed about the floor and crowded with additional spectators and participants. The President and many members of his Cabinet were in attendance, as were other important government officials and dignitaries, when Mr. Philip Phillips, the thirty-one-year-old gospel singer, was introduced as the guest soloist of the evening. Seated at his little portable organ which was placed directly in front of the platform on which the desks of the presiding officers stood, the man who had been lovingly nicknamed "The Singing Pilgrim" after the success of his illustrated songbook based upon John Bunyan's "Pilgrim's Progress," began by singing "Your Mission," by Gates and Grannis.

Lincoln was so deeply impressed by the song and the manner in which the singer presented it, favoring particularly stanzas four (If you cannot in the conflict) and five (If you cannot in the harvest), that he quickly wrote a note to the Chairman of the Commission who was presiding that night, the Secretary of State, Honorable William H. Seward (during whose term of office the United States purchased Alaska from Russia, a deal which led his political opponents to dub the eventual forty-ninth state "Seward's Folly") "Near the close let us have 'Your Mission' repeated by Mr. Phillips. Don't say I called for it. A. Lincoln." (That brief note became a prized possession of the Phillips' family, being regarded as a "rare relic.") The singer acceded to the Presidential request, and from that hour on "Your Mission" was spoken of as the favorite hymn of Mr. Lincoln, although it was actually more of a sacred song than a Christian hymn, being neither "addressed to nor descriptive of one of the Persons in the Holy Trinity."

While Daniel March "Christianized" the idea of "Your Mission" in his later hymn, the singer himself said of the song, "The charm of the composition consists in its pure Gospel Spirit. The teaching of Christ is touchingly embodied in the verses; the music is admirably adapted to express the inmost meaning of the truth conveyed." It was later that same year that the singer sent the poet a request that she versify one passage in Bunyan's "Pilgrim's Progress" which dealt with Christian's dream of the holy city. Mrs. Gates sent him the stanzas entitled "The Home Of The Soul." Phillips read the familiar passage from Bunyan to his little son, and then, after reading the requested stanzas, immediately felt the inspiration to compose the music. Taking his pencil in hand, he turned to his little organ and wrote the tune, later making this observation, "This hymn seems to have had God's special blessing upon it from the very beginning." Ira D. Sankey, who was inspired to become an evangelistic

singer by "The Singing Pilgrim's" example and advice, sang
this song over the composer's grave in Fredonia, New York,
thirty years later.

Mrs. Ellen H. Gates wrote many more poems before her
death in 1920 at the age of eighty-five (a volume of her works,
"Treasures of Kurium," being published in 1895) and Mr.
Grannis composed many more popular songs, and Mr.
Phillips gave many more concerts and song services—one in
Selma, Alabama, being attended by Jefferson Davis, the ex-
President of the Confederate States of America—and com-
posed many more sacred tunes before the Lord called him
home in 1895, but the labors of the three of them together
made possible "Your Mission," the favorite hymn of President
Abraham Lincoln.

GENERAL ROBERT E. LEE'S FAVORITE HYMN

General Robert Edward Lee (1807-1870) was a devoutly
religious man whose virile Christian faith undergirded his
every act, in war as well as in peace. He who is quoted as
having said that "duty is the sublimest word in the English
language" drew spiritual strength from The Holy Bible, and
to the best of his ability, lived out its precepts in his own
daily life. "No one ever becomes too old to study the precious
truths of the Bible," he once told the college students at
Washington College (now Washington and Lee University,
Lexington, Virginia) and at family prayers every morning
before breakfast, passages from The Bible were read, for
Lee regarded The Holy Scripture as "a book which supplies
the place of all others, and cannot be replaced by any other."

Even during the bloody years of the Civil War, Lee always
held himself above bitterness and hatred, and on one occasion
he said to a group of young women, "I believe I may say,

looking into my own heart and speaking as in the presence of God, that I have never known one moment of bitterness or resentment." When, in 1853, his daughters expressed their desire to be received into full membership in the Protestant Episcopal Church, General Lee himself renewed his vows of Church membership, being inspired as much by the beautiful faith of his wife as by the decision of their daughters. After the war, when he accepted the Presidency of Washington College in Virginia, he continued to set an example to his students by attending Church services regularly, his seat in the College Church being in the second pew from the pulpit, directly in front of the chancel.

Like his famous comrade in arms, General Stonewall Jackson, Lee gave Almighty God the glory for every military victory and continued to believe in the beneficence of his Heavenly Father in hours of sorrow and sadness. One of his biographers says of him, "He could not have conceived of a Christian who was not a gentleman," and a Christian was one who never shrank from doing his duty, regardless of how difficult or distasteful it might be. "There is a true glory and a true honor," he often said, "the glory of duty done, the honor of the integrity of principle." At 9:30 o'clock on the morning of October 12, 1870, after an illness of two weeks, General Robert E. Lee died at his home in Lexington, Virginia. Two days later, at 9 o'clock on the morning of October 14, 1870, eulogies were delivered by three well-known clergymen, Rev. W. S. White, Rev. J. William Jones and Rev. Dr. Pendleton. The body lay in state throughout that day, and on the following day, October 15, committal services were held and his body delivered to its final earthly resting place.

Many of the men who had marched with him and fought under him during the years he commanded The Army Of Northern Virginia came down from their mountain homes to pay their last respects to their honored and revered leader. Those who had invaded the north with him, only to be stopped at Gettysburg, as well as many of those who, under his inspired leadership and superb strategy, had routed the Federal invaders during the Seven Days Battles near Rich-

mond, and at Fredericksburg, Cedar Mountain, Chancellorsville and many a lesser battlefield, trooped into Lexington
to pay him their final homage, while those who had wept
with him at Appomattox stood in silent tribute to their
fallen hero. Many of these tattered veterans of one of the
world's noblest armies stood in small groups about the college
campus while others marched by his coffin in the chapel
nearby, weeping openly and unashamedly at the passing of
one of their nation's few genuine Christian noblemen. Then,
when all of the eloquent tributes had been fittingly spoken
and the last echo of the last voice had died away, somewhere
a soldier began to sing a selection they all knew was the
General's favorite, and soon others took up the strains and
still others, until the heavens resounded with the stirring
stanzas of the hymn which Lee had requested be used at his
funeral "as an expression of his full trust in the ways of the
Heavenly Father":

1. How firm a foundation, ye saints of the Lord,
   Is laid for your faith in his excellent word.
   What more can he say than to you he hath said,
   To you who for refuge to Jesus have fled?
2. In every condition, in sickness, in health,
   In poverty's vale or abounding in wealth;
   At home and abroad; on the land, on the sea—
   "As thy days may demand, shall thy strength ever be."
3. "Fear not, I am with thee, O be not dismayed,
   For I am thy God and will still give thee aid;
   I'll strengthen thee, help thee, and cause thee to stand
   Upheld by my righteous, omnipotent hand."
4. "When through the deep waters I call thee to go,
   The rivers of woe shall not thee overflow;
   For I will be with thee, thy troubles to bless
   And sanctify to thee thy deepest distress."
5. "When through fiery trials thy pathway shall lie,
   My grace all-sufficient shall be thy supply;
   The flame shall not hurt thee; I only design
   Thy dross to consume and thy gold to refine."
6. "E'en down to old age my people shall prove

My sovereign, eternal, unchangeable love;
And when hoary hairs shall their temples adorn,
Like lambs they shall still in my bosom be borne."
7. "The soul that on Jesus still leans for repose,
I will not, I will not desert to his foes;
That soul, though all hell should endeavour to shake,
I'll never, no never, no never forsake."

The authorship of these magnificent stanzas remains a mystery to this very day, although they have been variously ascribed to such hymn writers, musicians and poets as Keith, Kirkham, Kingsbury and Keene, all of whom figure in the puzzling history of this superb singable statement of a sterling, stalwart Christian faith. George Keith, a London publisher and book-seller, was a son-in-law of the distinguished clergyman, Rev. Dr. John Rippon, who included "How Firm A Foundation" in the 1787 edition of his book of sacred songs, while Robert Keene was the man who served as Musical Director of the Baptist Church in Carter Lane, Tooley Street, London, during Dr. Rippon's pastorate, which began in 1773 and lasted for sixty-three years, until his death in 1836 at the age of eighty-five. Just who Kirkham and Kingsbury were, hymnologists have been unable to determine and these four men got into the picture only because Dr. Rippon signed these remarkable stanzas with just the letter "K," which leads to all sorts of speculations as to the correct identity of the author. Since Robert Keene, Rippon's precentor, composed the tune to which these lines were originally sung, more than likely he is the man to whom the honor is due. Rippon's collection, fully entitled "A Selection of Hymns from the Best Authors, Intended as an Appendix to Dr. Watts' Psalms and Hymns" proved so immensely popular that three years after their first publication in London, they were being reprinted for use in Baptist Churches in the United States, and while the Anglican (Established) Church never included the hymn in any of its official hymnals, several of these stanzas may be found in nearly every other denominational hymn in English-singing Christendom.

The two tunes to which they are now generally sung are

the old, early American camp-meeting tune, "Foundation," which more than likely was the one used at General Lee's funeral, and the "newer" tune, "Adeste Fidelis," composed in 1751, the music to which the Christmas processional hymn of praise, "O Come All Ye Faithful," is universally sung. This latter piece of music is sometimes known as "Portuguese Hymn," not because it came from the country of that name, but because it was used regularly in the Portuguese Chapel of one of England's historic cathedrals, and in the Chapel of the Portuguese embassy in London. The most important facts, however, regarding the words and music of "How Firm A Foundation" are not whether we will ever know the true names of the author and composer, but the certainty that, whoever they were, they knew "Him of Whom they sang," and it was for this reason and this alone, that the hymn was the favorite of President Theodore Roosevelt, that it was sung by request during the last and fatal illness of President Andrew Jackson and that it was a full and complete expression of the dynamic faith of General Robert Edward Lee.

GENERAL STONEWALL JACKSON'S FAVORITE HYMNS

General Thomas Jonathan (Stonewall) Jackson (1824-1863) knew he did not have much of a voice for singing, but that did not deter him from joining his fellow-Christians in praising God by means of psalms, hymns and spiritual songs. Morning and Evening prayers were part of the daily schedule and routine of his camp, and the singing of hymns was as much a part of worship as the reading of the Scriptures or the offering of verbal petitions to the Almighty, and often Jackson's "toneless voice" could be heard singing some of the hymns he loved the best. One particular favorite of his was written by Rev. Charles Wesley (1707-1788), the co-founder of the Methodist Church, in the year 1749, to express the joy of the happy convert and contained these lines in the first, second and fifth stanzas:

1. (O how happy are they) Who the Saviour obey
   And have laid up their treasures above!
   Tongue can never express The sweet comfort and peace
   Of a soul in its earliest love.
2. That sweet comfort was mine When the favor divine
   I first found in the blood of the Lamb;
   When my heart first believed, What a joy I received,
   What a heaven in Jesus's Name!
3. O the rapturous height Of that holy delight
   Which I felt in the life-giving blood!
   Of my Saviour possessed, I was perfectly blest,
   As if filled with the fulness of God.

The genuineness of Jackson's conversion was evident in the way he practiced his Christianity, even in the midst of the pressing duties of war. After the victorious Valley Campaign, he sat down in his tent and wrote his pastor back in Lexington, Virginia, a letter to this effect, "My dear pastor, In my tent last night, after a fatiguing day's service, I remembered that I had failed to send you my contribution for our colored Sunday School. Enclosed you will find my check for that object, which please acknowledge at your earliest convenience, and oblige yours faithfully, T. J. Jackson."

When General Bee attempted to rally his frightened and scattered forces at the First Battle of Manassas (Bull Run), July 21, 1861, he shouted to his men, "There is Jackson standing like a stone wall. Rally around the Virginians," and from that moment on, the professional soldier and West Point graduate who had been a Professor at Virginia Military Institute in Lexington, Virginia for ten years prior to the outbreak of hostilities, was respected, loved and feared as Stonewall Jackson. Yet, in his heart he must have been conscious of the years of his own spiritual rebellion, for in two of the hymns he loved the best and sang the most, the word "rebel" occurs. In the fourth stanza of Wesley's hymn "O How Happy Are They" are these words, "He hath suffered and died, To redeem a poor rebel like me," while the second line of the first stanza of his other favorite contains the plea, "Let a repenting rebel live." This second hymn came from the pen of the British divine, Rev. Isaac Watts (1674-1748) and is his versification of David's great hymn of penitence, Psalm Fifty-One. In Watts' monumental work, "The Psalms of David Imitated in the Language of the New Testament and Applied to the Christian State and Worship," first published in 1719, and popular enough to be re-published a century later, the preacher-poet included five different hymns inspired by passages taken from the Fifty-first Psalm, containing a total of thirty-two separate stanzas. The first hymn, captioned "A penitent pleading for pardon" had six stanzas, all of which had endeared themselves to the brilliant military strategist, for often he could be heard singing in his "vocal monotone" these words from Watts, as if he had long since made them his very own:

1. Show pity, Lord; O Lord, forgive; Let a repenting rebel live;
   Are not thy mercies large and free? May not a sinner trust in thee?
2. My crimes are great but can't surpass The power and glory of thy grace;
   Great God, thy nature hath no bound, So let thy pardoning love be found.
3. Yet save a trembling sinner, Lord, Whose hope, still hovering round thy word,
   Would light on some sweet promise there, Some sure support against despair.

The only other hymn which those who knew Jackson ever remembered him singing was Hymn 418 in the 1843 edition of Psalms and Hymns prepared for use in Presbyterian Churches. The General himself had united with the Lexington Presbyterian Church on November 22, 1851, at the age of twenty-seven. This hymn of three stanzas was written by the eccentric British genius, man-of-letters and hymn writer,

William Cowper (1731-1800) and dated 1773. As the first hymn in the section of the hymnal entitled "Submission Under Trials," Cowper of Olney had penned these auto-biographical lines:

'Tis my happiness below Not to live without the cross;
But the Saviour's power to know, Sanctifying every loss.
Trials must and will befall; But with humble faith to see
Love inscribed upon them all, This is happiness to me.

Jackson, who earned international renown and undying fame in the Valley Campaign of 1862, always attributed his military triumphs to a beneficent and all-wise Providence, never hesitating to invoke the blessings of God upon his arms or to thank the Lord for having afforded him a victory. With General Robert E. Lee he fought in the Seven Days Battles that lifted McClellan's siege of Richmond and drove the Federal invaders back down the Virginia peninsula to Harrison's Landing on the banks of the James River far from the Confederate capitol. Later, they fought side by side at Cedar Mountain, Antietam and Fredericksburg. But it was at Chancellorsville, in May, 1863, that the genius and daring of the two men forged a victory that will live forever in military annals. When General Jackson outlined his strategy to General Lee, whose depleted forces faced a Federal host that out-numbered them two to one, the latter asked him simply, "General Jackson, what do you propose to do?" Pointing to a map and to a recently discovered route that would take him behind the enemy's right flank, he answered calmly, "Go around here." Lee then asked, "What do you propose to make this movement with?" to which Jackson replied, "With my whole corps."

At 5:15 p.m. that fateful May 2, 1863, Jackson and his whole corps were in place behind the enemy, and the charge under General Rhodes that soon routed and destroyed the Federals was begun. By night fall victory was assured. Later, in the darkness, as the Commanding General and some of his staff were returning from a scouting mission, they were mistaken for enemy soldiers and fired upon by their own men, Jackson suffering a severe wound in his left arm. Near midnight he was finally taken to a field hospital at Wilderness Old Tavern and his physician summoned. When Lee sent him a note congratulating him upon the glorious victory, the wounded Jackson whispered, "General Lee is very kind but he should give the praise to God." On May 4 he was moved further to the rear, to the Chandler home near Guiney's Station on the Richmond-Fredericksburg-and-Potomac Railroad, in the hope that he could recuperate more rapidly farther from the field of battle, especially in view of the fact that his wounded left arm had recently been amputated. The news of this tragedy brought forth from General Lee this remark, "General Jackson has only lost his left arm; I have lost my right arm!"

On May 7, his doctor realized that his patient had developed pneumonia, and Mrs. Jackson was brought to his bedside from her temporary home in nearby Richmond. On Saturday night, May 9, 1863, the feverish soldier asked his wife, Anna, to sing with him some of the hymns he loved so well. Soon he was joining her in the stanzas of Watts' hymn, while those in the room who knew the words sang aloud with them, and others who recognized only the tune hummed it softly:

Show pity, Lord, O Lord, forgive; Let a repenting rebel live;
Are not thy mercies large and free? May not a sinner trust in thee?

Before they reached the last stanza, Jackson's lips were moving but his voice was almost inaudible. The following day, Sunday, May 10, 1863, after his physician had notified him that he would soon be in heaven, he whispered, "Yes, I prefer it; I prefer it. It is all right."

Then, as the evening drew nigh, he added, "Let us cross over the river and rest under the shade of the trees" and marched out to cross the Jordan and meet his Maker.

HE LEADETH ME

During the first year of the Civil War, things did not go well at all for the northern armies. Those political leaders who thought that the whole conflict would be victoriously prosecuted and successfully terminated within two or three short months were facing the grim prospect of a long drawn-out, costly, destructive war, that could drag on for years, and from which the country, united or divided, might never completely recover.

General McClellan fully expected to lead his Army Of The Potomac straight down the highway from Washington to Richmond when he mustered his men to meet the Confederates under General Beauregard at Manassas Junction in northern Virginia that fateful July 21, 1861. But, due in most part to the stalwart bravery of General Thomas J. Jackson, who earned his nickname "Stonewall" that very afternoon, the invader was routed with a loss of fifteen-hundred men. Although the defenders counted nearly two-thousand casualties when the sun set over the battlefield of Bull Run that evening, they knew that they had snatched a dramatic victory from the jaws of certain defeat and that the day was truly theirs!

For the first time, those who had goaded their leaders to make irresponsible threats and inflammatory accusations, as well as those who had encouraged the actual outbreak of hostilities, realized what they had set in motion and what they, as well as the entire country, were in for! The rest of that first year, 1861, saw no other great movement of large armies as each General tried to out-think, out-smart and eventually out-maneuver his opponent.

But early in 1862, as the second year of the conflict began, General Ulysses Simpson Grant gathered his Union forces and set out to take or destroy two Confederate strongholds, Fort Henry on the Tennessee River and Fort Donelson, not too far away on the Cumberland River, knowing that if he reduced those defensive positions or forced their "unconditional surrender," Kentucky and a large part of Tennessee would be lost to the Confederacy. On February 6, 1862, Grant defeated General Buckner and won the first important Union military victory at Fort Donelson, leaving twenty-five hundred casualties on the field to two-thousand for his adversary. This frightful toll of irreplaceable human life shocked the sensitive people on both sides of the Mason-Dixon line and many shuddered to think what was yet in store for the Blue and the Gray if the war continued very much longer at that terrible rate! Then, just a month after Grant's initial success in the west, the Confederate ironclad, *Merrimac* (re-christened the *Virginia*) slid from her berth and began to wreak havoc with Federal ships in Hampton Roads. Since that fleet held the key to McClellan's success or failure in his current drive on Richmond via the Virginia peninsula, where he had already landed an army of more than one-hundred thousand men, fear again gripped the States of the Union, as people wondered how long their helpless wooden navy could withstand such disastrous assaults and such mortal blows. Just in the nick of time, the Union ironclad, Ericson's *Monitor*, a "cheese box on a raft," appeared in the same waters to defend McClellan's life-line, and the two engaged in the first battle of ironclad ships in the history of naval warfare, March 8, 1862, a slugfest that resulted in a tie, since neither side could claim a complete, untarnished victory. But the shudder that swept through the seaport cities of the northern states did not subside with the news of the struggle that had been joined in Virginia waters, and many frightened citizens fully expected a fleet of iron vessels to appear in their harbors at any moment to bombard them, lay their cities waste, or blow them all to Kingdom come!

Against that background of defeat, disappointment, disillusionment and despair, a twenty-eight-year-old Baptist clergyman, Rev. Joseph Henry Gilmore, conducted a midweek prayer service in Philadelphia's downtown First Baptist

Church on the corner of Broad and Arch Streets on Wednesday night, March 26, 1862. Boston-born on April 29, 1834, and an honor student at Rhode Island's Brown University, from which he graduated in 1858, Gilmore entered Newton Theological Seminary to complete his training for the Christian ministry. After he received his Bachelor of Divinity degree from Newton in the late spring of 1861, he supplied various Baptist Churches in different cities for almost a year before accepting a call from a Baptist congregation in Fisherville, New Hampshire, where he was ordained later the next year, 1862. Thus it was that the Gilmores were in Philadelphia that spring, the clergyman supplying the pulpit of that historic Church for several weeks. The minister took as his theme for the mid-week service Psalm Twenty-three, and spoke at length on "God's leadership," dwelling for some time on the various meanings to be discovered in the simple phrase "He leadeth me" which occurs twice in the first three verses of the Shepherd Psalm. He brought out further the "blessedness of being led by God" as well as "the mere fact of His leadership, altogether apart from the way He leads us" or "what He was leading us to" as well as from or out of. If ever such a message was needed by a group of faithful Christian people, it was that Wednesday night in March, because the war into which they had entered so joyously a year before had bogged down into a murderous and deadly serious business that appeared to have no immediate end. And, just as ministers in the south were encouraging their people to "endure hardship as good soldiers of Jesus Christ," so northern preachers were attempting to bolster up their people's low spirits by assuring them of God's leadership throughout the prolonged night of battle, closing on the confident note of eventual victory which, they assured their hearers, He would grant them in His own good time!

At the close of the service, the Gilmores were guests in the home of Deacon Wattson and his wife who lived right next door to the Church. Among other Church leaders who dropped in for a chat with the supply pastor and his wife were Mr. and Mrs. Washington Butler. Soon all of them were discussing the message of the evening, and commenting upon its appropriateness at that particular time, especially in view of the circumstances of the hour and the conditions confronting the Union during those perilous spring days. Quite casually, as all of them were enjoying some light refreshments and visiting informally, the young minister took out a piece of paper and began to jot down some lines that came into his mind and heart. Although the others in the room were unaware of what he was doing, his wife kept her eyes upon him, and later smiled knowingly when he slipped the piece of paper into her hand. Glancing down, she read the four simple four-line stanzas that he had written, inspired by the enthusiastic response of the people to his brief meditation of the evening:

1. He leadeth me! O blessed thought!
   O words with heavenly comfort fraught!
   Whate'er I do, where'er I be,
   Still 'tis God's hand that leadeth me.

2. Sometimes 'mid scenes of deepest gloom,
   Sometimes where Eden's bowers bloom,
   By waters still, o'er troubled sea—
   Still 'tis His hand that leadeth me!

3. Lord, I would clasp thy hand in mine,
   Nor ever murmur nor repine;
   Content, whatever lot I see,
   Since 'tis my God that leadeth me.

4. And when my task on earth is done,
   When, by thy grace, the victory's won,
   E'en death's cold wave I will not flee,
   Since God through Jordan leadeth me.

Chorus:

He leadeth me, He leadeth me,
By His own hand He leadeth me;
His faithful follower I would be,
For by His hand He leadeth me.

Unknown to the preacher-poet, Mrs. Gilmore saw the devotional possibilities in the simple stanzas and sent a copy to the editor of the Boston Baptist publication, "Watchman and Reflector." He published them in the issue of December 4, 1862, and when the composer William B. Bradbury (1816-1868) found them in the columns of that journal, he immediately set them to music, as he had previously set to fine singable tunes such hymns as "Jesus Loves Me," "Sweet Hour Of Prayer," "On Christ The Solid Rock I Stand," and "Just As I Am Without One Plea." The new hymn was published for the first time in Bradbury's collection of Sunday School songs entitled "The Golden Censer" in 1864.

Strange as it seems, Gilmore did not know what his wife had mailed or what Bradbury had composed until he went to Rochester, New York in 1865 to preach in the Second Baptist Church of that city. President Anderson of the Divinity School took him to the Church where he was scheduled to speak the day after his arrival, and, as the service began, Gilmore thought, "I wonder what they sing," opening the hymnal and discovering to his utter amazement that they were singing his own hymn, "He Leadeth Me." He explained his reaction to that dramatic moment later when he said, "I shall never forget the impression made upon me by coming in contact then and there with my own assertion of God's blessed leadership."

The Gilmores went to Fisherville, New Hampshire, after their brief stay in Philadelphia, and, following his ordination, the minister served the Baptist congregation there for one year. When his father, Joseph A. Gilmore, was elected Governor of the State, young Joseph served two years, 1863 and 1864, as the elder Gilmore's private secretary. The next two years found him serving the Second Baptist Church in Rochester, after which he taught Hebrew in the Theological Seminary in that city. In 1868 he became Professor of Logic, Rhetoric and English Literature in Rochester University, filling that post with distinction for more than forty years. Six books and many more poems came from his pen prior to his retirement in 1911, none of which enjoyed the universal and well-merited popularity that "He Leadeth Me" received.

Eight years after the preacher-poet-professor died at the age of eighty-four in 1918, the United Gas Improvement

Company purchased the building and dwelling formerly occupied by the First Baptist Church and the Wattsons on the corner of Broad and Arch Streets in downtown Philadelphia, and, while the Church and house were being demolished by professional wreckers to make room for a spacious new office building, a Baptist clergyman of the city said to a company official, "That old building has a remarkable history. A wonderful hymn 'He Leadeth Me' was written there."

When the new edifice was completed, a bronze tablet was erected and formally dedicated, commemorating the event that had taken place sixty-four years earlier on that very same spot. The plaque, placed on the Arch Street side of the new building, bears this inscription:

> "He Leadeth Me," sung throughout the world, was written by Rev. Dr. Joseph H. Gilmore, a son of a Governor of New Hampshire, in the home of Deacon Wattson, immediately after preaching in the First Baptist Church, northwest corner Broad and Arch Streets, on the 26th day of March, 1862. The Church and Deacon Wattson's home stood on the ground upon which this building is erected. The United Gas Improvement Company, in recognition of the beauty and fame of the Hymn, and in remembrance of its distinguished author, makes this permanent record on the first day of June, 1926.

The only original bugle call to come out of the Civil War was "Taps," reputedly composed by the Union General, Daniel O. Butterfield, at Harrison's Landing, on the James River in Virginia, in July, 1862, while McClellan's defeated army was waiting to be taken aboard Federal vessels and shipped back to Washington, following the Seven Days Battles and General Robert E. Lee's lifting of the siege of Richmond. But the only sacred hymn that came out of the four-year conflict was "He Leadeth Me," and it is worthy of noting in conclusion that had each side seriously and sincerely sought God's Divine leadership before they became too deeply involved in faulty political solutions, and too irretrievably committed to temporary and destructive human devices, "blind leaders leading the blind," no doubt the controversy that erupted into war could have been averted and the "peace of God" in human hearts as well as in human society could have been preserved.

HERITAGE AND HOPE

When the Civil War began in April, 1861, and men and boys began to say "Goodbye" to their loved ones and march off to a war that was supposed to last only three or four weeks at the most, one or two composers turned out one or two patriotic songs which they considered worthy of the occasion. But as month gave way to weary month and year to dreary year, more and more composers, the talented as well as the untalented, got into the act, and by the time Lee and Grant got together at the McLean House in Appomattox, Virginia on Palm Sunday, April 9, 1865, more songs had been written than during any other American war before or since, and the remarkable thing about some of them is that they still retain their popularity even after the passing of a hundred years, while many of the war songs of intervening conflicts have long since been fortunately forgotten.

While the south was appropriating an Ohio minstrel man's song written up in New York State, "Dixie," and making it its very own, the north was taking over a Georgia camp-meeting tune and refrain, "Glory, Glory Hallelujah!," composed by a Richmonder, and making it their "Battle Hymn Of The Republic."

Some mediocre songs enjoyed temporary fame but soon faded from sight as better ones were written and published, but, in general, those from the southern states could not hold their own with those from the northern states. This was not because of their subject matter, for no subject could be more thrilling than the defense of one's beloved homeland against an armed invader, unless it be the personal majesty of General Robert E. Lee or the boldness of General Stonewall Jackson or the daring of General Jeb Stuart. But many of the most popular southern songs suffered from melodies that were contrived and forced rather than inspired, and musical progressions that were almost too trite to put down on manuscript paper, as well as from a monotonous sameness that stamped them as the work of the same composer or of the same school of musical training, or as poor imitations of earlier successes.

When George F. Root's "The Battle Cry Of Freedom" was published in Chicago in 1861, a southern version was soon rolling from the presses in Nashville and Memphis, while southerners who were better patriots than they were poets, dashed off Confederate stanzas for "The Star Spangled Banner" as well as fiery lines to be sung to the music of the French national anthem, "The Marseillaise." Even the tunes of the prolific composer-publisher Armand Edward Blackmar somehow fail to "come off," lacking that ring of sincerity which is an integral although sometimes an intangible part of every successful patriotic song, even though he had such stirring stanzas as Father Ryan's "The Sword Of Robert E. Lee" and Henry St. George Tucker's "The Cross Of The South" to work on.

Both sides were equally alert in drafting "God and the right," and their warlike verses are pathetic examples of the perversion of true religion to serve the particular causes which one faction happens to hold dear at a given moment. Clergymen and laymen turned out poems with equal ease, while women tried their skill at it and proved themselves the equals if not the superiors of the men, beating them at their own game! Carrie Bell Sinclair of Georgia versified "Strike For The South," "The Homespun Dress" and its sequel "The Soldier's Suit Of Gray," Mrs. C. D. Elder exalted the glory of "The Confederate Flag," Catherine Warfield of Kentucky wrote "The Southron's Chaunt Of Defiance," and Julia Crawford wrote "Kathleen Mavourneen" which became a southern wartime "hit," while other women did their literary best to romanticize the war as Elizabeth Browning had romanticized romance! Boston-bred Julia Ward Howe's

"The Battle Hymn Of The Republic" easily outshone the songs of every other Yankee with the sole exception of George Frederick Root, while Ethel Lynn Beer's sentimental story "All Quiet Along The Potomac" or "The Picket Guard" was as big a tear-jerker as the songs of the Confederate composer Charles Carroll Sawyer, whose works included "Weeping Sad And Lonely," "The Faded Coat of Blue" and the dying soldier's lament, "Who Will Care For Mother Now?".

How some of the poorer songs ever got published will remain forever a mystery, as will the fact that some of the better songs failed to interest some of the more astute business men of the day who were afraid to risk their money on the fickle musical tastes and preferences of a nation divided by fratricidal strife. When Walter Kittredge failed to find a publisher for his sad and doleful song, "Tenting Tonight On The Old Camp Ground," he proceeded to popularize it himself by singing it wherever he went. Surprisingly, his buddies liked it and puzzled publishers knew that the frustrated composer had the last laugh on them!

North and South vied for the honor of producing the best songs, each knowing that its finest productions would be almost immediately appropriated by the other and adapted to his particular needs. So there came the martial airs that sent a quiver down the spine and the melancholy songs that brought a tear to the eye, and, since suffering and sorrow were universal, and knew no limits of time or space, the sad songs were sung by the boys in blue as well as by the boys in gray, neither one caring whether they had been composed by Yankees or Confederates or first published in Chicago or New Orleans. Thus "Lorena" became the sweetheart of both sides, since those who fought under both flags shared that experience in common.

While General Grant is reputed to have said that he knew only two tunes, one was Yankee Doodle and the other wasn't, other military leaders knew the value of music and encouraged their men to sing together the songs that were dear to their hearts. During those four bloody years, Hart Pease Danks, whose tunes for the hymn "No Night There" and the song "Silver Threads Among The Gold" are perennial favorites, composed a Memorial Day tune for a poem entitled "We

CARL A. RUDISILL LIBRARY
LENOIR RHYNE COLLEGE

Deck Their Graves Alike Today," while C. C. Converse, whose best hymn tune was composed for Joseph Scriven's stanzas "What A Friend We Have in Jesus," brought out a briefly popular sentimental song at the same time, "The Rock Beside The Sea." As for William B. Bradbury, whose splendid tunes for "Jesus Loves Me," "He Leadeth Me," "Sweet Hour Of Prayer," "Saviour Like A Shepherd Lead Us" and the invitation hymn "Just As I Am Without One Plea" are among the finest in Christendom, he dashed off a song that became a great favorite with the Army Of The Potomac, entitled "Marching Along." Since President Lincoln appointed new Generals for this army almost every time the moon changed, Bradbury wisely made his Chorus easily adaptable to every alteration:

> Marching along, we are marching along,
> Gird on your armor and be marching along;
> McClellan's our leader, he's gallant and strong,
> For God and our country we are marching along!

Bradbury also took a cue from Root and brought out his own version of "Rally Round The Flag" which couldn't hold a candle to the former composer's, since it contained such "forced rhymes" as these:

> Rally round the flag, boys, Give it to the breeze;
> That's the banner we love, On the land and seas.
> Brave hearts are under ours, Hearts that heed no brag,
> Gallant lads, fire away! and fight for the flag!

One can see almost immediately why that song didn't have too long a musical life! For a while "answer songs" became all the rage, and could have been sung antiphonally by armies camped on either side of the Rappahannock, the Mississippi or the James. "Paul Vane" was written as an answer to "Lorena." John Hill Hewitt's "When Upon The Field Of Glory" was a Confederate reply to Yankee Sawyer's "When This Cruel War Is Over." Hewitt also composed music for "The Picket Guard," "Somebody's Darling" and "Rock Me To Sleep, Mother," as well as such songs as "The Young Volunteer," "The Soldier's Farewell" and "We Are Going To

The Wars, Willie Boy," none of which outlasted the reconstruction days.

James Pierpont, whose Christmas ditty "Jingle Bells" is now a universal December favorite, tried his hand at it and composed tunes for "We Conquer Or Die" and "Strike For The South," little dreaming that his Christmas song would outlive them by more than a century! As for Benjamin Russell Hanby, whose "Darling Nellie Gray," "The Uncle Tom's Cabin of song," had been written and composed in 1856 while the young man was still a college student, he also wrote "Ole Shady, The Song Of The Contraband" which is found only in collections of Civil War songs now, while his lovely Christmas hymn "Who Is He In Yonder Stall" is sung on both sides of the Atlantic, and is more popular in England today than in his native United States. Harry MacCarthy, a prolific though shallow versifier, had an inspiration when he read that after South Carolina had seceded from the Union she adopted as her new banner a blue flag bearing a single star in the center. His new song appeared almost simultaneously with the new flag and swept through the southern states like a prairie fire, although it lacked the grandeur and grace of "Rally Round The Flag, Boys" which is better known as "The Battle Cry Of Freedom." MacCarthy's stanzas contained these lines:

1. We are a band of brothers and native to the soil,
   Fighting for the property we gained by honest toil.
   And when our rights are threatened, the cry rose near
      and far,
   Hurrah for the bonnie blue flag that bears a single star.

Chorus:

Hurrah, hurrah, for southern rights hurrah.
Hurrah for the bonnie blue flag that bears a single star.
2. As long as the Union was faithful to her trust,
   Like friends and like brothers, kind were we and just;
   But now when northern treachery attempts our rights
      to mar,

We hoist on high the bonnie blue flag that bears a single
   star.

3. First gallant South Carolina nobly made the stand,
   Then came Alabama who took her by the hand.
   Next quickly Mississippi, Georgia and Florida,
   All raised the flag, the bonnie blue flag that bears a
   single star.

4. Ye men of valor gather round the banner of the right,
   Texas and fair Louisiana join us in the fight.
   Davis, our loved President, and Stephens, statesmen are;
   Now rally round the bonnie blue flag that bears a single
   star.

5. And here's to brave Virginia! The Old Dominion state,
   With the young Confederacy at length has linked her
   fate.
   Impelled by her example now other states prepare
   To hoist on high the bonnie blue flag that bears a single
   star.

6. Then cheer, boys, cheer, raise the joyous shout,
   For Arkansas and North Carolina now have both gone
   out;
   And let another rousing cheer for Tennessee be given,
   The single star of the bonnie blue flag has grown to be
   eleven.

7. Then here's to our Confederacy; strong we are and
   brave,
   Like patriots of old we'll fight, our heritage to save;
   And rather than submit to shame, to die we would
   prefer;
   So cheer for the bonnie blue flag that bears a single star.

Harry sang this new song in September, 1861, at the Varieties Theatre in New Orleans, to the tune of an old Irish jig "The Jaunting Car" and next to "Dixie," it became the best-loved song of the seceding states. In fact, General "Beast" Butler, who earned his nickname by the cruel way he ruled New Orleans after its capture by the Yankees, imprisoned the song's publisher and threatened to levy a $25 fine on any one he heard singing it, a small fortune in those desperate days! MacCarthy capitalized on the fame of his first success by following it up with "The Volunteer" or "It Is My Country's Call." Unfortunately Harry was neither conscripted nor did he ever volunteer to defend that bonnie blue flag, claiming British citizenship to escape combat and finally fleeing north when the Confederacy collapsed.

Parodies and sectional versions of this and other songs became increasingly popular as the war dragged agonizingly along, humorous and sarcastic stanzas coming along just in time to lift the soldier's morale and give him the added zest he needed to muddle his way through one more gory battle. While some of the tunes have long since died away, the music to which the northerners sang:

> Old Abe Lincoln came out of the wilderness, Many long
> years ago,

was being sung during the First World War to a ditty that began:

> "Uncle Sammy, he's got the infantry, he's got the cavalry,
> he's got artillery,
> And when we all get over to Germany, Goodbye Kaiser
> Bill."

"The Yellow Rose Of Texas" which serves as theme or background music for many contemporary motion pictures and television shows built upon the real and mythical exploits of Civil War heroes, was actually a darkey's sweetheart, according to one version which had this line in its Refrain:

> "The sweetest rose of color this darkey ever knew,
> Her eyes are bright as diamonds, they sparkle like the
> dew";

but the song became popular with both whites and darkeys as the war progressed, and "The Yellow Rose" became the "back-home sweetheart" of reluctant conscripts as well as radiant and recently-released slaves.

Nearly every great military victory was soon memorialized in a new song, while the leading heroic personages on both sides came in for their share of poetic glory. Hymns as well as jigs, and minstrel melodies as well as gospel songs abounded on both sides of the Mason-Dixon line, while even the un-

95

known honored dead were immortalized in song and story before the final shot was fired and terms of surrender agreed upon and signed. Although "When Johnny Comes Marching Home" is said to have been written during this period by "Beast" Butler's bandmaster, Patrick Sarsfield Gilmore, it "came into its own" during the Spanish-American war in the last decade of the nineteenth century and is now generally considered, along with "A Hot Time In The Old Town Tonight," one of the distinctive musical contributions of that brief conflict.

While the centennial of the Civil War will undoubtedly see a revival of many of the songs that were dear to the hearts of combatants and civilians both north and south, the passing of time cannot dim the lustre of the truly great songs of that era nor can it add any to those mediocre ballads that had their day "and then ceased to be." "America," written by Rev. Samuel Francis Smith in 1832, almost thirty years before the firing on Fort Sumter, and "The Star Spangled Banner" by Francis Scott Key which antedates "My Country 'Tis Of Thee" by eighteen years, and "America The Beautiful" penned by Katharine Lee Bates in 1892, twenty-seven years after Appomattox, have now supplanted most of the Civil War hymns and songs in the hearts of the American people, although "The Star Spangled Banner" did not officially become the national anthem until 1931, when President Herbert Hoover signed a Congressional bill to that effect. Nevertheless, since two of these three were peace-time productions penned by people with virile Christian backgrounds and upbringing, we can take heart in the knowledge that the truly sterling songs of the United States do not need a war for their inspiration but are the products of peace instead. As long as the holy light of freedom burns on the altars of American hearts, we can continue to invoke the blessings of a beneficent Providence upon our beloved homeland in the words of the Baptist divine who prayed:

> Long may our land be bright
> With Freedom's holy light;
> Protect us by Thy might,
> Great God, our King!